GTR MANCHESTER VOL I

Edited by Steve Twelvetree

First published in Great Britain in 2003 by
YOUNG WRITERS
Remus House,
Coltsfoot Drive,
Peterborough, PE2 9JX
Telephone (01733) 890066

All Rights Reserved

Copyright Contributors 2002

HB ISBN 0 75434 223 9
SB ISBN 0 75434 224 7

FOREWORD

This year, the Young Writers' The Write Stuff! competition proudly presents a showcase of the best poetic talent from over 40,000 up-and-coming writers nationwide.

Young Writers was established in 1991 and we are still successful, even in today's modern world, in promoting and encouraging the reading and writing of poetry.

The thought, effort, imagination and hard work put into each poem impressed us all, and once again, the task of selecting poems was a difficult one, but nevertheless, an enjoyable experience.

We hope you are as pleased as we are with the final selection and that you and your family continue to be entertained with *The Write Stuff! Gtr Manchester Vol I* for many years to come.

CONTENTS

	Scott Broome	1
	Katrina O'Neill	1
	Daniel Kilbride	2
	Danielle Gorton	2

Booth Hall Hospital School

	Kirsty Ledger	3
	Oliver Fitton	4
	Alyson Booker	5
	Rosie O'Shea	5
	Robert Whalen	6
	Briony Donnelly	7
	Amy O'Connor	8

Cardinal Langley RC High School

	Lucy Branagan	8
	Daryl Booth	9
	Rachel Rooney	10
	Alanya Coop	10
	Sophia Fenlon	11
	Michael Beisty	12
	Rachael Carey	13
	Rachel Dawson	14

Harrop Fold School

	Luke Walker	14
	Zoe Wrigley	15
	Kelly Whitworth	16
	Jenna Foster	16
	Naddine Burke	17
	Lisa Parsonage	17
	Abbey Neilan	18
	Daryl Bratt	18
	Emma Hedley	19
	Lee Edge	19
	Hayley Flynn	20

Gemma Chapman	20
Jade Smith	21
Jordan Baxter	22
Samantha Tomlinson	22
Craig Jones	23
Danielle Dewsnip	23
Michael Flaherty	24
Ruby Burdaky	24
Danielle Edge	25
Joshua Parker	26
Danielle Horsefield	26
Rebecca Batey	27
Hannah Graham	28
Hannah Walsh	28
William Bestwick	29
Jessica Crispin	29
Micheal Smith	30

Irlam & Cadishead Community High School

Andrew Jones	30
Emily Stones	30
Caroline Yates	31
Adam Neal	31
Daniel Price	32
Thomas Bannister	32
Leanne McCormick	33
Ashley Duplex	33
Andrew Jackson	34
Chelsea Andrew	34
Josh Lynch	35
Leanne Farnworth	35
Jennifer Brickhill	36
Matthew Swindells	36
Helen Moulder	37
Steven Coward	37
Amy Flanagan	38
Rebecca Keymer	38
Judy Foster	39

	Samantha Rook	39
	Samantha Wilson	40
	Samantha Davies	40
	Michael Dodd	41
	Rachel Massey	41
	Danielle Sanderson	42
	Joanne Heaton	43
	Karla Kirton	44
	Danielle Rotin	44
	Ruth Bradford	45
	Jenna Whitelegg	45
	Craig Underwood	46
	Owen Meehan	46
	Johnathon Royle	47
	Dawn Whitehead	47
Lancasterian School		
	Bobby Fallarino	48
	Frank Lee	48
Newall Green High School		
	Zoe Louise Mulvihill	48
	Stephen Collins	49
	Vanessa Atherton	50
	Lucy Gill	51
	Matthew Campbell	52
	Matthew Neild	52
	Craig Rigby	53
	Daniel Boyle	54
	Natalie Chapman	54
	Danielle Preston	55
	Michelle Roscoe	56
	Paul Daly	57
	Daniel Telfer	58
	Carl Brady	58
	Nicola Fox	59
	Jamie Price	59
	Hannah Willis	60

Leanne Petit	60
Rebekah Hill	61
Amany El-Sayed	61
Nathan Brookes	62
Jayne Cookson	63
Natalie Braddock	64
Anthony Fox	64
Terry Lee	65
Kimberley Sutton & Simone Humphries	66
Caroline McGovern	66
Farah Hussain	67
Elizabeth Nixon	68
Chloé Brelsford	68
Natalie Grimsley	69
Stephen Hutchinson	70
Jake McNicholls	70
Matthew Wilde	71
Megan Cole	72
Emma Murphy	72
Laura Marino	73
Laurence Wardle	73
Melissa Green	74
Jason Whitwell	74
Aaron David Fairhurst	75
Lee Matthews	76
Roisin Cryan	76
Victoria Ludden	77
Lois Farrar	77
Ryan Done	78
Charlotte Cordingley	78
Hannah Cummings	79
Kieran O'Hare	79
Daniel Finlay	80
Stephanie Downing	80
Louise Towse	81
Stephanie Taylor	81
Marcus Ely	82
Melissa Tennant	82

Name	Score
Rebecca Lowe	83
Tanya Suddons	84
Jason Kane	85
Simon Peak	85
Lucas Billingham	86
Joshua Howarth	86
Laura Hampson	87
Holly Candlin	87
Selina Farrington	88
Leanne Price	88
Jennifer Duff	89
Anthony Law	89
Daniel Holt	90
Jessica Jarratt	90
Mark Harrop	91
James Davenport	92
Nicola Hewitt	92
Laura Carbert	93
Amy Herbert	93
Lee McGuinness	94
Wayne Hobbs	94
Michael Crosse	95
Adam Taylor	95
Natalie Simpson	96
Aimee Benn	96
Heather Anderson	97
Rochelle Williams	97
Jenny Bruton	98
Robert Miller	99
Stephanie Green	100
Dale Davies	100
Wade Loose	101
Stephanie Brennan	102
Kelly Jones	103
Rebecca McWhirter	103
Kevin Long	104
John Gaynor	104
Sam Dunbar	105

Sam Middleton	106
Katie Lehane	106
Rio Walker	107
Megan Miller	108
Brent Macauley	108
Daniel Williams	109
Jenny Day	109
Craig Thompson	110
Jessica Mulvey	110
Aiden Billingham & Kayleigh	110
James O'Brien	111
Alana Oven	111
Aaron Holmes	112
Cheryl Kane	112
Lewis Herbert	112
Nathan Gilbert	113
Warren Capper	113
Sara Eastwood	114
Robert James Bates	114
Leanne Berry	115
Jamie Morris	115
Karen Burt	116
Sarah Walker	116
Nichola Parry & Shadelle Logan	117
Dean Hardie	117
Anna Hoy	118
Rachel Molloy	118
Louise Parkes	119
Jodie Armstrong	119
Ashley Nunn	120
Rachael Taylor	120
Leigh Townsend	121
Rosie Joanne Edwards	121
Sarah Barclay	122
Jacqueline Smith	122
Aston Hughes	123
Danielle Palin	123
Sam Morris	124

David Burns	124
Racheal McCoy	125
Hannah Rimmington	125
Matthew Taylor	126
Daniel Miller	126
Jordan Harrison	127
Lee Stevenson	127
Bradley Thomas	128
Rebecca Wovenden	128
Sam Thomas	129
Craig Bell	129
Aaron Creighton	130
Tiffany Connor	130
Rea Holly Hickman	131
Aaron Lyons	131
Laura Molloy	132
Chelsea Agoglia	132
Darren Horsfield-Eaves	132
Adam Pate	133
Arron Finch	133
Jack Hawksworth	134
Stephen Bird	134
Amelia Rigby	134
Reon Davies	135
Becky Sefton	136
Clare Welch	136
Kelsey Latimer	137
Samantha Farrar	138
Thomas Haspell	138
Vicky Hindley	138
Chloé Boswell	139
Sophie Herstell	139
Klodjana Hasi	140
Joe Farrar	140
Jenna Deveney	141
Victoria Gough	142
Jade Dawson & Emma Burns	143

Swinton High School
> Vicki Bootman 144
> Nicola Burke 144
> Vikki Jones 145
> Sharron Cheetham 146
> Christopher Ogden 147

The Poems

SEPTEMBER 11TH

We wake up each morning
To greet a new day,
Not knowing what cruel things
Are coming our way.

Out of the sky like a bird with wings,
The sound intense, ears started to ring.
It flew into the building with one terrible rage,
Not many poor souls on this day were saved.

The sound was loud, the sky burning bright,
Those planes were never going to ever take flight.

In the streets below, the dust was thick,
Gathering unbelievably quick.
People were running to and fro,
Not knowing where to turn or go.

The day then ended with great dismay,
As a lot of lives were lost that September day.

Scott Broome (15)

UNTITLED

Don't ever mess with Katrina
She's a nasty sort of girl
She's got powers like Sabrina
My best mate is called Tina
My set in school is pearl.

Katrina O'Neill (12)

A Tall Story? Yes, That's Right

This is a tall story about me, Dan. I would like to be a giant, as if I was in the rainforest trying to reach for the light. Yes, that's right, I am a tree standing there in a lonely meadow all by myself, just all alone by myself in a meadow watching the grass grow, no one there to bother me.
I want to go up to the clouds soaring and breaking them up! Yes, that's right, I'm a bird flying above the sky looking from the clouds at the big, busy city.
I want to creep over the horizon like a great ball of fire, yes that's right. I am the sun giving everyone a lovely tan. I travel all around the world faster than anything goes, I am always around.
I would like to write stories that rhyme, yes that's right.
I would like to be a poet describing my feelings in what I write. I would also like to win awards for the best teenage poet of the year. I want to make people joyful and entertain them, yes that's right.
I would like to be an entertainer opening people's hearts with fun, acting funny as if I was in the shoes of a clown, being daring enough to step in the shoes of a lion tamer. I would like to go places and tell people what I have wrote. Yes, that's right, I am Daniel!

Daniel Kilbride

My Mate The Biker

A biker I know has brown curly hair,
He's big and gruff and tends to stare.
He has bad habits that he won't give in,
He's old and lazy, he has a stubbly chin.

He rides around on his swanky bike,
Revs the engine and flashes the lights.
The exhaust pipe stalls, it's a piece of old tatter,
The engine falls out, oh what a clatter.

He thinks he's cool dressed in all his leathers,
But if you tell him different he loses his tether.
He thinks it's fashionable to wear black shades,
He's a fashion disaster and needs to be saved!

He's quite funny and laughs at his own jokes,
He eats like a warthog and nearly chokes.
He'll always help you, he's got smelly feet,
That's my mate, the biker, whose name is Pete!

Danielle Gorton (13)

SUNNY, OUR SHETLAND

Sunny, our Shetland, munches in the moor
Stumbling and falling all over the floor,
Lingering near the tack room
Is it time for tea?
Yes it is
Stop neighing at me!

He wolfs it down in one second flat
Then I put him in the paddock
And give him a pat.
He rolls in the mud, then shakes where he's stood,
I'm bringing you out
No need to shout!
I'll put on your rug, then give you a hug
Now I'll go home
And leave you alone.

Kirsty Ledger (13)
Booth Hall Hospital School

STAR WARS RAP

Come on everybody, let's hear you clap,
We're gonna do the Star Wars rap.

With all the gang and the Death Star too,
Solo, Chewy and Skywalker's crew.

Come on everybody, let's hear you clap,
Han is doing the Star Wars rap.

Leia is the funky diplomat,
But she don't wear no silly hat.

Come on everybody, let's hear you clap,
Luke is doing the Star Wars rap.

Vader is the dark and evil one,
He used to be good but now that's gone.

Come on everybody, let's hear you clap,
Vader's doing the Star Wars rap.

Luke's the Jedi with the big plan,
No one will cross him cos he's the man.

Come on everybody, let's hear you clap,
We've now done the Star Wars rap.

Oliver Fitton (12)
Booth Hall Hospital School

WINTER

Winter sneaked
Through the quiet countryside
Covering the earth with soft white snow
Turning the water into ice
Making it shine and glow.

Winter crawled
Through the dark, sleepy town
Spreading a white blanket
Over the sparkling rooftops
Making them shine and glow.

Winter dashed
Through the freezing forest
Covering the trees with gleaming frost
Turning the waterfalls into blocks of ice
Making them shine and glow.

Alyson Booker (11)
Booth Hall Hospital School

MY CAT FARO

My cat will never complain or whine
He's always just fine
He once ate the washing line
But he was still fine
He drank two bottles of wine
But he was still fine
He stole some food of mine
I hit his nose but he still felt fine
But when a fly landed on his tail
You could really hear him wail!

Rosie O'Shea (13)
Booth Hall Hospital School

ALPHABET ANIMALS

Alex the anteater can tell the time
Bob the buffalo does a good mime

Carrie-Ann the camel wears a hat
Diane the dingo strokes her cat

Emma the eel slips through the net
Fiona the frog makes a good pet

Gary the giraffe knits a new sweater
Harriet the hippo receives a long letter

Isobel the iguana has a good dance
James the jaguar slips into a trance

Kate the kangaroo reads a long book
Lonnie the leopard likes to cook

Mandy the mongoose likes to rumble
Nicholas the newt lives in the jungle

Oscar the owl works all night
Percy the penguin likes to fight

Quentin the quail likes to run and run
Rachel the rabbit eats a cream bun

Sarah the snake plays football
Thomas the tortoise dances in the hall

Ursula the unicorn washes her car
Vicky the vixen is a big star

Willie the whale can swim for miles
Xavier the xtra-terrestrial always smiles

Yvonne the yak caught fish in a sack
Zelda the zebra gives rides on her back.

Robert Whalen (13)
Booth Hall Hospital School

SPRING

Spring rises
Through the outside world
Waking up the flowers
Telling the trees to blossom
Blowing away the winter.

Spring comes
In winter's place
She turns the trees green
Bringing new life
And blesses the world with her gentle touch.

Spring glides
Above the shivering sea
Gently warming up the waters
Stirring her magic
Into the waves below.

Briony Donnelly (14)
Booth Hall Hospital School

MY LITTLE SISTER

My little sister is such a pain,
She loves to play out in the pouring rain.
Splashing about with her wellie boots on,
I preferred it when the sunlight shone.
My little sister is such a pain,
She always wants to play with my game.
She often ends up breaking it,
Then I have a great big fit.
My little sister is such a pain,
Which really is a crying shame.
But I know deep down she truly cares,
Even if she doesn't show it,
My little sister!

Amy O'Connor (12)
Booth Hall Hospital School

JEALOUSY

Jealousy is like a seed,
That plants itself within your mind,
Watered by envy it grows,
Thoughts constricted by its twisted roots.
Powered by anger, jealousy flowers,
Its unfolding leaves bursting with spite,
Stalked by generosity, jealousy is ripped out by the roots,
But remnants of its existence linger in the dark recesses of our fertile minds.

Lucy Branagan (13)
Cardinal Langley RC High School

SCARLET BLOOD: PURPLE HEARTS

Boats barge onto the shore
Soldiers dying more and more
On the beach and on the land
In the mud and on the sand
Snipers here, snipers there
Look around, they're everywhere
Take them out, shoot them down
We've taken over this whole town
Carry our wounded, bury our dead
There's not much more that can be said.

As we've taken over this town
Our rifles high, our spirits down
We start to pack, prepare to leave
We're in the air, so we believe
As a man starts to complain
We lose control of the aeroplane
Reaching Britain was a relief
Blood was pouring from our chief
Our chief grew pale, he almost died
The troops rejoiced when he survived.

As we dress up fine and smart
We really try to look the part
As the major calls out our name
Proudly we walk to the stage
He shows his hand, a glimpse of gold
A shiny medal he does hold
As they listen to his speech
All the widows start to weep
Instead of having to duck and dive
We stand and wear our 'hearts' with pride.

Daryl Booth (13)
Cardinal Langley RC High School

THE BULLY

He looks at me and he sees red,
Sometimes I wish that I were dead.
An everlasting game of cat and mouse,
I want to hide out in my loving house.
He gets me behind a gathering crowd,
Nobody hears because it's too loud.
He snatches my dinner money, kidnaps my snack,
If I don't give in then he'll give me a smack.
Alone in this world, like one pea in a pod,
My hope is fading, oh please help me God.
Is it because I wear glasses or because I am too small?
Nobody knows, nobody cares and nobody hears my call.
Does he have problems at home, maybe with his mother?
He makes my life hell, so why should I bother?
All that I know is, I wish it would end,
I can't tell a soul, not even my friend.
Without him, my problems would be left behind,
I'm sure that there can't be two of his kind.
I can be strong; I can get my own back!
Beware Tony Cooper, I'm planning *attack!*

Rachel Rooney (13)
Cardinal Langley RC High School

THE BULLY

She's there.
Her destructive glare. Those unripe eyes.
I am sealed to the floor.
She's coming this way.
Her sooty, black boots team with her tangled hair to reinforce my panic.
Is that my heart beating?
I daren't glance at her as she approaches.

One bad move can prove ill-advised.
'The money!'
My trembling hand dives into my pocket and pulls out a note.
The *Queen* appears to be frowning at me.
Satisfied, the creature slinks away, leaving a scar
not visible to the human eye.
She's gone. I sigh.
She's gone.

Alanya Coop (13)
Cardinal Langley RC High School

THE BULLY

She's so lonely,
Her feelings have been locked up
and the key thrown away.
She is forever in debt,
Giving away her daily paper round money
in an instant,
Just for taking a breath.
She dreads laughter,
It might be them.
Her eyes are forever dashing from
side to side.
She constantly sees traffic lights;
Red meaning she's in danger, they have arrived,
Amber meaning the bullying has begun,
And finally green, they've seen a teacher,
they're backing off.
She relaxes for just a moment, breathes a sigh
and begins to hope again
that they will have forgotten her by tomorrow.

Sophia Fenlon (13)
Cardinal Langley RC High School

THE BULLY

He towered over me,
like a skyscraper in Manhattan,
His robust shell defended him,
from my feeble attempts of attack.

His eyes glowed red with rage,
His big fists were clenched tighter
than a python constricting its prey,
I was the victim, his prey.

With one huge almighty blow,
he knocked me over,
like dropping a stone off a bridge,
I curled up in a ball.

The crowd around me laughed and jeered,
I started to cry,
The bully would not stop,
it was like he was in a kicking frenzy.

After he'd stopped, the last words he said,
Stayed ringing in my head,
When his face was so red,
'Fight, here, tomorrow, 6 . . . '

I hope tomorrow never comes.

Michael Beisty (13)
Cardinal Langley RC High School

IF ONLY . . .

A tentative peek around the corner,
There is no one to be seen,
I breathe once again.
Nervously, glancing around, as if a startled deer,
I emerge from the safety of the forest into the open plain.
A cold breath is on the back of my neck.
I whirl around, face to face with confrontation.
'Going somewhere?'
Those two icy words give me a chill from head to toe.
My hands start to shake as my heart plummets to my feet.
'I think someone wants to give me a present.'
His voice is dripping with sweetness, yet I am terrified.
'I h-haven't g-got it,' I whisper.
'What?'
'I h-haven't got it,' I say wincing, waiting for the punishment.
'Where's my money?'
He snarls like a rabid dog, his face close to mine.
Suddenly, a tide of angry words rush to my mouth,
But at the last moment before they spurt out, I lose my nerve.
The tide flows back out, my fear returns.
A torrent of pain flows through me.
My arm is wrenched behind me.
'Have it by tomorrow!' he hisses. 'Or else!'
As the vice is loosened, I flee,
Tears prick my eyes.
Why didn't I stand up to him?
I'll do it next time . . .
I *will* do it next time . . .
I will.
Won't I?

Rachael Carey (13)
Cardinal Langley RC High School

THE JOURNEY OF A POEM

I am nothing but a speck in your mind,
But then I expand.
I send a message to your hand,
Telling it to write.
Blank lines begin to fill,
As a letter,
A word,
A descriptive sentence.
You look at me in discontent,
You don't like what I say.
Angry and disappointed,
You rip me into pieces.
I once was an idea,
Brilliant and clever,
But now I am nothing more
Than shattered pieces of your frustration.
Your idea has been torn,
So I exist no more.
I could have been great,
With a little more work,
But now in the bin I wait
For your next poem mistake.

Rachel Dawson (13)
Cardinal Langley RC High School

DEATH CAMP

Young men cry,
Their wives and children die.
Pulling out their own teeth
And shaving each other bald.
The Jews have fallen.

No chance of escape,
You die when you touch the gate.
You're forced to eat bread and water
And you have to share a bed.

Luke Walker (11)
Harrop Fold School

GHOUL SCHOOL

When we were in school
I spotted a creepy ghoul.

I carried on with my work
Sitting next to Kirk
When I spotted it again.

I got up from my seat
And started to do a beat.

'Oh, if you're here now, ghoul,
In this boring old school
Please show your face,
Or I'll knock you through the wall.'

The ghoul showed up
And said, 'I'm sorry.'
But I said, 'Don't worry.'

Me and the ghoul became best friends
And ended up as a good story ends.

Zoe Wrigley (11)
Harrop Fold School

LEFT HERE ALONE

No more pain,
Finally I am away
From the cold, wet nights
My family are gone
I'm left here alone
If I had a choice
They'd still be here.

Only if we didn't go
It made it worse
I had to move their bodies
And burn them
My son, my only son has gone.

I hated the work
My wife and son were weak
They should have taken me.

Kelly Whitworth (12)
Harrop Fold School

MY BROTHERS

Oh brother!
They're as bad as each other.
Lee plays with Sean's gun
And it ends up Sean has to run.
But other nights,
They fight with all their might.
They gang up on me
On silly things like how to make Mum's cup of tea.
But at the end of the day it's only Sean and Lee,
And they still love the family and, of course, me!

Jenna Foster (12)
Harrop Fold School

DANCING

Moving freely with my arms
In all kinds of directions
Flicking my feet out like I'm a ballerina
I hear the beat of the music
Coming from all over the place
As I feel the air
Brush along my face
I think of Heaven beside me.

I feel fantastic
As I move my body
I feel like a bird
Floating
As I begin to think of a song
I begin to hum
As the beat takes over.

Naddine Burke (12)
Harrop Fold School

PE

PE, PE is the best
I will beat all the rest
Even if you think it's crummy
I may become a teacher and get loads of money
I like it best when running a race
Even if the wind blows up in my face
I love to hear the gun go *bang*
My heart is pumping, it goes *clang*
I try not to let out my aggression
Because it is the end of the lesson.

Lisa Parsonage (16)
Harrop Fold School

IF I MET A CELEBRITY

I would love to meet a celebrity,
Let's say . . . Victoria Beckham.
I'd say hello
And ask about Romeo.
I'd feel all shaky
Just in case I said something silly.
I'd ask for her autograph
And show all my friends,
I'd brag about it forever,
But . . .
I don't think I will meet her after all.
But there's no harm in dreaming
And anyway,
Who said dreams don't come true?

Abbey Neilan (11)
Harrop Fold School

THE GALE

He banged and bellowed with anger
angrily tearing the broken, brown gate
from its rusty hinges.
Bin lids and litter fighting frantically
in the rough, windy war.
He viciously flung down slates
from the garage roof.
The defenceless tree was attacked
by this unique storm.
The wind, squawking with anguish
like a weeping child.
As the clouds moved and laid a carpet
for the moon to take over.

Daryl Bratt (12)
Harrop Fold School

LISTEN

I'm standing in the classroom,
Waiting for someone to hear,
I'm shouting at the top of my voice,
I'm filled with fear,
Let me out, let me out.

I'm here, I'm here,
No need to shout,
They said to stop crying,
No need to grouch.

I close my eyes
As I take in the pain,
I want to tell them,
I need them to listen,
The anger inside me
Makes me want to explode.

It's over, it's over,
No need to cry,
They said it's OK now
That you are all friends.

Emma Hedley (12)
Harrop Fold School

WHAT AM I?

I travel to different places, there and back
I stop in different places all over the world
I am very tall and long
I have wings on me
I take people on holiday
Do you know what I am?

Lee Edge (11)
Harrop Fold School

MY DREAMS

I would go to sleep,
Not making a peep,
I'm flying high like an aeroplane
With wings on my back,
Flying so high, not leaving a track.
I could be in danger,
Or asleep in a manger,
I could be chased by things,
Maybe something with gigantic wings.
I could be filled with fear,
Then I hear,
Some noises so loud,
Not being heard in millions of crowds.
Then suddenly I see a big beam
And then I realise and wake from my dream.

Hayley Flynn (12)
Harrop Fold School

MY FANTASY DOG

My dog is great,
He's only a puppy, but he's a fantastic mate.
My dog is crazy and bubbly and is always there for fun
And my, oh my, he can run.

My dog is really good,
He likes getting dirty in the mud.
My dog likes to play all the games I play,
Sometimes there aren't enough hours in the day!

My dog is called Ben and he is mine,
It's like living on cloud nine.
But there's one thing about my dog that I need to tell you,
He lives in my dreams and isn't true.

Gemma Chapman (11)
Harrop Fold School

GALE

Gale got out of his bed this morning
He put on his scarf and slammed the door
Today was his favourite day of all
A day of terrorising his neighbours
He sneaked around the corner
And with one mighty puff
He blew the hat off a snowman
The snowman looked at Gale with his button eyes
And turned away in disgust.

Gale had a smug look on his face
Looking for more mischief
Sun appeared
To give Gale a lecture
Sun shone her glistening rays
Sweat trickled off her face
Gale sulked and drifted back to his house
To wait for the next season to come.

Jade Smith (11)
Harrop Fold School

THE MONSTERS IN MY ROOM

There's vampires in the wardrobe
And monsters under the bed
Then there are the ones on the ceiling
Who just pretend they're dead
There's werewolves under the table
And spiders in the drawers,
But the scary thing about them
Is they all have huge teeth and claws
All these scary monsters, they are all in my room
Some walk about, some are in cocoons
Some of these monsters can fly
Some of them can swim
But my favourite one of all
Is the rainbow-coloured one called Jim.

Jordan Baxter (12)
Harrop Fold School

HOLIDAYS

I love to go on holiday
And swim in the sea,
I love the warmth of the sun
Burning my skin,
I love the taste of ice cream
Melting in my mouth,
I love to go on holiday
With my family.

Samantha Tomlinson (13)
Harrop Fold School

FREEDOM

What is freedom?
Is it where you are free from the grasp of Hitler?
Free from torture?
Free from slavery?
Free from Hell?
I am free from all of these,
But still I don't feel free.
They killed my wife and baby girl,
I was made to shave my wife's beautiful golden hair,
I was made to shave my daughter's shiny hair
And I was made to melt the wedding ring my wife was wearing.
No wonder I don't feel free.
I am trapped in grief.
Freedom is where you are safe and happy.

Craig Jones (11)
Harrop Fold School

GRANNY

I have a really groovy granny.
We went to the shops
To get some lamb chops
And my best mate spotted me.

I have a really groovy granny.
We went on some rides
I wanted to hide
She is really embarrassing.

I have a really groovy granny.
She wears diamonds and pearls
And a T-shirt with swirls
I love to be with Granny!

Danielle Dewsnip (11)
Harrop Fold School

HALLOWE'EN

Ghosts 'n' ghouls freed at last
Scaring children at night
All around the world.
They hide in different places,
Even underground.

There are ghosts in the graveyard
There are bats in your hair
There are vampires in the chimney
They are small and some are big.

But all the monsters are only trying
To make the most of their only night
So why don't we all do the same
And scare people to death.

All night long deafened by screams
But night soon comes to an end.
Now it's morning and we're all bored
We have to wait another year
Until we can frighten again.

Michael Flaherty (12)
Harrop Fold School

ZOO TROUBLE

I went to the zoo
Around quarter past two
With my mum and dad
And my brother, called Drew.

We spotted a monkey crawling up a tree
And then it looked back and it must have spotted me!
The giraffes were chewing leaves, reaching with their long necks
One reached down and took my dad's specs!

We went to the birdhouse and had a root around
One was really loud and made an awful squeaky sound
'I do not want a bird,' I said to my dad,
'I also have a brother and that's already bad.'

So we made our way home on the motorway
My mum said, 'Guys, have you had a good day?'
My dad looked for his glasses and started to groan
And when he found them we started to make our way home.

Ruby Burdaky (12)
Harrop Fold School

YOU ARE A RAINBOW

When I look at you
I see a rainbow.

Your eyes are as blue
as the sky.

Your cheeks are as red
as a rosebud.

Your hair is golden
like sand.

Your skin is like
peach velvet.

When I think of you
I see a rainbow.

When it rains and the sun comes out
you are watching over me.

Danielle Edge (12)
Harrop Fold School

I Wish

I wish I was him,
I wish I wasn't born.
He had everything - friends, money
And I didn't know why.

The jealousy took me over,
I couldn't stop it,
I was like a disease.

But now everything will be alright,
I will have it all
And he won't because
I will take it.
I will be him,
I will do it.
He will die, no longer exist
And I will do it.

Joshua Parker (12)
Harrop Fold School

Monday Morning Blues

Monday morning
I get out of bed
Feel like there's a hammer
Inside my head.

Get dressed
Just like Mum said
I feel like a bull
When it sees red.

I haven't a disease
Or a bad flu
It's simply a case
Of Monday morning blues.

Danielle Horsefield (11)
Harrop Fold School

FRIENDSHIP

I've lots of friends
In my school
They all care for me
And I do too.

They make me laugh
And we all have fun
Together each day
In the playground and at home
We have lots of fun.

When we all go home
From a hard working day
The fun goes on
Throughout the day
I love having friends.

We all have secrets
That we would never tell
We trust each other
Every day and on other days
That's what friends are for.

Rebecca Batey (12)
Harrop Fold School

WEATHER

I opened my front door and what did I see?
Frosty skies in front that made me shiver on one knee.
I closed my eyes and murmured and shivered in the cold,
I waved to my friend across the road, then I walked in my home.

I opened my front door and what did I see?
The snow was falling from the skies and landing on my knee.
Then to my surprise my sister came running down the stairs
And bumped into me.

I opened my front door and what did I see?
The rain was falling very hard and spitting at me.
I knelt down on my knees and stared at the sky,
It was such a marvellous sight in my very bright blue eyes.

Hannah Graham (12)
Harrop Fold School

MY DREAM

I dream of being an athlete
Like a cheetah bolting after its prey,
On your marks, my body starts to shake,
Get set, the ground beneath me trembles.

To compete in the Olympic stadium
Which roars like a giant hurricane,
Feeling like a jaguar
Waiting to pounce on its tasty prey.

With the winning medal around my neck,
Glistening like a golden gem,
Tears of joy fall onto the medal,
The race is over, I am the *champion*.

Hannah Walsh (11)
Harrop Fold School

NOBODY

You're nice on the outside,
But never mind, you still hate me,
But from now on
I'm going to be king of the rockers,
I'm going to be as mean as you,
It's like looking into a mirror,
You're less intelligent than a skateboard,
You've an intellect
Only rivalled by garden tools,
Even the shed.
You will see,
I will rule,
You will drool,
You cheerleader.

William Bestwick (12)
Harrop Fold School

FRIENDS

Friends are like your family
They give you advice
Share all your secrets
And are always nice.

I have loads of friends
But only one is the best.
She can talk,
She is my best friend.

I have a best friend,
She is fab.
She helps you when you are stuck,
That is my best friend.

Jessica Crispin (12)
Harrop Fold School

MY GRANNY

My granny is old,
So very old,
The oldest person there is to behold.
But she parties all night,
Which gives my mum a fright,
Until the morning when she wakes up yawning.

Micheal Smith (12)
Harrop Fold School

MY DOG

I have a little dog called Sam,
He is soft and cuddly, like a little lamb.

Getting old now, but still he pleases
And shakes his head every time he sneezes.

He acts like a king, demanding everything,
But he's still a cute little thing, that's Sam.

Andrew Jones (13)
Irlam & Cadishead Community High School

MY RABBIT

She's soft and cuddly,
Fluffy and white.
Her eyes brighten on a starry night.
Her old age shows
Through the aching of her bones.

Emily Stones (12)
Irlam & Cadishead Community High School

TO THE USA

A sheet of dark velvet crossed the sky,
Mothers and babies began to cry.
Broken hearts were lost forever,
Because someone thought they were very clever.
Under the black rubble people lie,
Hoping that they'll live, not die.
Workmen and firemen digging in the dirt,
Searching for people badly hurt.

Thousands of innocent lives were lost,
Wonder how much money it'll cost?
Lots of people wandering around,
Wishing that relatives had been found.
For some this wish didn't come true,
USA, this poem is for you.

Caroline Yates (14)
Irlam & Cadishead Community High School

MEN AND WOMEN

Men are tall
Women are small
Women show their feelings and men don't
Women bloom like a flower in the summer
Men keep themselves to themselves
Women share their troubles and are like an open book
Men are like a locked up diary.

Women have no shame in crying, they could fill the seas with tears
Men can only fill their eyes with tears.
This is the difference between men and women.

Adam Neal (12)
Irlam & Cadishead Community High School

ALIEN - DIFFERENCE POEM

As the shiny star shot across the sky,
A green domed head popped up,
Out came its spiny fingers,
Its webbed feet, as it crawled out.
Its skin as green as grass.
It stood up and looked through its sparkly eyes,
With a different sort of smile,
It toddled along the ground,
Acting like it was drunk.
Then its back cracked open,
Two broad wings popped out.
It jumped and flapped then flew up towards the sky
Then swooped down and landed.
It waddled towards the shadows . . .

Daniel Price (12)
Irlam & Cadishead Community High School

EMBRACING RACE

Race, in your face.
Every day, it's here to stay.
People let loose,
With torrents of abuse.
How it hurts me
They don't know.
It hurts bad
And makes me so sad.
So let us not judge by colour or race,
And please just get out of my face.

Thomas Bannister (12)
Irlam & Cadishead Community High School

HANNAH

Hannah is cool,
but she is a fool,
Hannah is funny,
just like a bunny,
She likes spaghetti Bolognese,
and she cares for me always.
She is always there for me,
as fast as a bumblebee,
She has brown hair
just like a fluffy bear.
Hannah drinks rum,
showing her bum,
when she eats food,
she always gets rude,
but all I can say is Hannah Kay
is the best!

Leanne McCormick (13)
Irlam & Cadishead Community High School

HEROES

H eroes are everywhere. In your street, in your house.
E very day people risk their lives to save another, or inspire someone else.
R esponding swiftly, which heroes do, they save lives and put things right.
O ver time people mature, creating a new breed of heroes.
E veryone can be a hero, saving lives like the heroes of today.
S o when you see a hero, remember they are your friend forever.

Ashley Duplex (13)
Irlam & Cadishead Community High School

DIFFERENCES

Who is different, you and me?
but that's the way it's meant to be,
those differences make you, you and me, me.

So what if we wear different clothes?
We're still the same inside.
And as most people know,
we should live to forgive and abide.

Colour black, white or brown,
It doesn't matter about colour,
it's what's inside that counts.
And almost everywhere you go,
you'll see someone that's different to you!

Andrew Jackson (12)
Irlam & Cadishead Community High School

MY TWIN COUSINS

Cute and cuddly,
is what they are.

Their cheeky smiles,
light up the room.

Their blonde hair
and blue eyes are
my favourite features.

Their kisses and cuddles
send a shiver down my spine.
I'll love them till my dying day.

My little Alfie and Annie.

Chelsea Andrew (12)
Irlam & Cadishead Community High School

DIFFERENCES

In the world that we do see,
Differences, there shall be.

Man or woman,
Black or white.
The racist battle,
We shall fight.

This cruel, selfish, hard time,
Things don't get better, but do decline.
How hurtful words can be,
When directed awfully.

I hope this poem gets through to you
And makes you think about what you do!

Josh Lynch (13)
Irlam & Cadishead Community High School

SOMETHING WE ALL NEED?

The one thing that everybody needs is love.
Thousands of loved people lose their lives.
Hope is for the people who survived
But not for the dead, no longer alive.
Among the graveyard people lie,
As their families cry.

The one thing everyone wants is peace,
A memory locked in our hearts forever.
A justice we all seek,
But love lives on through us all.
Let there be peace.

Leanne Farnworth (12)
Irlam & Cadishead Community High School

LOUISE

She is my shine,
My little princess.
She is my little
Louise,
She's cute, she's funny,
She's my apple pumpkin, my pudding pie.

She is the sunshine of my life,
She makes me happy
When skies are grey.

She is talented and gorgeous
My little lily pad
Her heart is pure,
Full with love and care.
She's my little
Louise.

Jennifer Brickhill (12)
Irlam & Cadishead Community High School

MY DOG

He is so cuddly,
But he is a dope.
He sits like a king
And he prowls like a lion.
He never barks, because he scares himself,
He covers the floor when he lies down.
He knocks me over
When he jumps up.
That is Homer, Homer my dog.

Matthew Swindells (13)
Irlam & Cadishead Community High School

TRUE LOVE

True love, a sweet-smelling rose
A warm vibrant feeling
A flower nurtured
Growing stronger
Lasting longer.

Left
It withers
Like pollen it can be passed
From one to another
Like a nerve it can be painful
A thorn causing pain.

Remember
Love is dangerous, it can hurt
But if you look after it,
It lasts forever,
Like a rose kept between the pages of a book.

Helen Moulder (15)
Irlam & Cadishead Community High School

TILLY, MY DOG

She thinks she's the boss,
But really she's soft.
She is quite funny,
She will give kisses,
She will protect me.
Although she is sweet,
She's really playful.
It's Tilly, my dog.

Steven Coward (12)
Irlam & Cadishead Community High School

MY POEM

In parts of the world there aren't children like you and me,
these children suffer.
They go through pain and torture each day,
they work for their families to keep them alive.
These children don't have much,
no food, no money and most of all, no education,
but what they do have a lot of is hunger and death . . .
There are people that escape all this,
but what happens to them?
It's all these riots on the street, the murder, the muggings,
and what does this come down to?
The colour of your skin . . . black or white.
What is this world we live in?
Is it this wonderful place where we all live in peace and harmony
or a place of destruction and chaos?
I ask you this,
what is it you want this world to be?

Amy Flanagan (12)
Irlam & Cadishead Community High School

MY HERO

My hero is kind and loving,
She is always there for me when I'm feeling down.
Cuddly and soft touching, she sits with me,
Honest is the way she always talks.
My hero, my mum.

Rebecca Keymer (13)
Irlam & Cadishead Community High School

RACISM

It's everywhere,
Spitting fire out of mouths.
Sticking up for yourself, if you dare
It makes me sick and others too.
Peace is what we need,
Not judgement, people do this too quickly,
It's everywhere, racism,
Don't do it as a dare,
We have not to stand and stare,
Peace is what we need
When are we going to have a thought
About the distraught?
Racism is everywhere
Black or white, I don't care.

Judy Foster (12)
Irlam & Cadishead Community High School

OLLIE

When I see him, I stand and stare,
He sits licking his soft brown hair.

He runs over and kisses me,
I sit down, he sits on my knee.

When I'm in trouble, he saves me,
When I'm happy, he plays with me.

So when I see him, I stand and stare,
I touch his warm, soft brown hair.

Samantha Rook (12)
Irlam & Cadishead Community High School

FLOWER

A friend in need,
is a friend indeed.
She makes me laugh
and giggles in class.
She's funny like a bunny
and eats lots of honey.
She wants to be a nurse
because she gets more money in her purse.
She's as loyal as a royal,
She goes to the fair.
with dazzling hair.
She climbs the tower
with her lucky flower,
She goes to the park in the dark.
She's a good friend,
now that's the end!

Samantha Wilson (12)
Irlam & Cadishead Community High School

ALL ABOUT MY CAT

He catches and scratches me
Like he is a busy bee.
He has a lot of fur
But he still likes to purr.
He likes his biccies
But sometimes they get tangled in his whiskers.
From morning till night we playfully fight.
At the end of the day we stop the play,
Then we go to bed instead.

Samantha Davies (12)
Irlam & Cadishead Community High School

MY MUM AND DAD

My mum and dad,
Brought me up as a lad
To do things the best way I can.

They'd give me a wash,
But now I want dosh,
To help me when I am a man.

As I grow older,
Get bigger and bolder,
I'll think of the things they have done.

The loving and caring
The teaching and sharing
All made my life so much fun.

Michael Dodd (12)
Irlam & Cadishead Community High School

DIFFERENT PEOPLE

All people are the same,
Fat or thin, they're not to blame.
The colour of people does not matter
Black or white
No need to fight.
Tall and quiet
Small and loud
Nobody should be ashamed
Everyone should be proud.

Rachel Massey (12)
Irlam & Cadishead Community High School

WHAT IS LOVE?

Love, what is love?
Is it all hearts and roses?
No.
Love causes pain and heartache.

Love is like a rose,
Starts off sweet and beautiful,
With heart-shaped petals,
But then you prick yourself on one of the thorns,
Causing you to break down and cry.

Love is never straightforward,
There's always something there,
To cause you pain,
To break your heart.

Love is like an onion,
You start peeling off the layers,
You think you are strong enough,
For the pain it may cause.

Some manage to get to the middle,
And in reward they get a ring,
But some cannot take the pain,
The tears, the heartache.
So they give up on it.

Is this love?
More pain than romance,
Passion and spice.
I suppose love is red,
Red for passion and romance,
Red for danger and pain.
Love . . .
Is this really what it is?

Danielle Sanderson (15)
Irlam & Cadishead Community High School

JUST A DREAM

I wish that there was no evil in this world of ours.
It's atrocious what can happen in a matter of hours.
I wish that nobody ever cried a single tear.
I wish that nobody had a single fear.
I wish that everyone had a smile on their face!
I wish that nobody would be sad if they lost the race.
I wish that our world would be happy and full of joy.
I wish that everyone got on, every man, woman, girl and boy.

I wish that you could look out of your window and see
A bright sunny sky, green grass and children full of glee.
I wish that the weather would always be sunny,
And everyone would be happy and funny.
I wish there'd be beautiful rainbows each day
And children could dance underneath them and play.
I wish that everyone was perfect, yet different too,
Then everyone would be happy, but not the same as you.

But the world is still filled with sadness and fear,
And drug addicts and alcoholics hooked on beer.
There are people who abuse, people who steal,
People who kill when behind a wheel.
There's rain and thunder, sadness and tears,
People each have their own different fears.

I dream of a world where things are different,
I dream of a world that is perfect and great,
I dream of a world where everyone agrees,
But I guess my dream will always be a dream.

Nothing more.
Just a dream . . .

Joanne Heaton (14)
Irlam & Cadishead Community High School

MY POEM

A single star in the sky,
A flower in the ground,
The most important things in life
Gone, gone, all gone.

When you lose someone,
Their pain has ended,
But the pain in our hearts will always go on because
The most important things in life are
Gone, gone, all gone.

Devastation flows through our minds,
Heartbreak and pain of all kinds.
It is hard to lose,
The most important things in life,
Gone, gone, all gone.

We have to be strong,
For they would not want us to sob.
We will remember them forever,
For the most important things in life,
Gone, gone, all gone.

Karla Kirton (13)
Irlam & Cadishead Community High School

FAMILY

Family is like the world,
It cannot be split in half.
You will be together, forever,
Like paper and pen.

Your eyes might be blue or green,
You may be black or white.
Your hair might be blond or brown,
You'll be all different heights.

Danielle Rotin (12)
Irlam & Cadishead Community High School

ROLO

Black and fluffy,
Cute and curly,
Big floppy ears,
Comes padding along.

Friendly and caring,
Playful and fun,
She's a Labrador cross poodle,
A Labradoodle!
And I love her.

Ruth Bradford (12)
Irlam & Cadishead Community High School

HOPE

Hope is something we need,
To get us through each day.
So for happiness we will pray,
Because we have each other.
And we have love,
So we can say,
That there is love on its way,
That is one thing that nobody,
Can ever take away.

Jenna Whitelegg (13)
Irlam & Cadishead Community High School

PETS: A TRUE STORY

I want a pet,
a cat maybe,
but surely not a dog
which my brothers will surely hog.

They come in different shapes and sizes,
but which one will I pick?
Just then I decided,
it's as small as a chick.

Black as night
as small as mice,
she looks at me with delight
I pick her up and she's so nice.

At home you'll surely see
she's the perfect cat for me.

Craig Underwood (13)
Irlam & Cadishead Community High School

DIFFERENCES

Everyone in the world today
black or white,
young or old,
rich or poor,
tall or short,
all are different,
but all have one thing in common,
all are human and have a place in the world.

Owen Meehan (12)
Irlam & Cadishead Community High School

FEELINGS

As we say a little something
good or bad
you might still feel really sad

Whether it's day
or whether it's night
you could be in for a real fright

Always be nice
always be kind
then you're guaranteed complete peace of mind

As we say a little something
good or bad
when is it time for us to be glad?

Johnathon Royle (12)
Irlam & Cadishead Community High School

A FRIENDLY POEM

Friends look out for each other,
Natasha is always there,
She gives me hugs when I am sad,
I can tell her anything,
She is trusting,
She loves chocolate and cheeseburgers,
She is my star friend,
She is my big sister.

Dawn Whitehead (12)
Irlam & Cadishead Community High School

FROM A TRAM WINDOW

Zooming, windy
High Street Station heaving with people
Buildings dawdling past
People dash.
On the tram, houses creep away
The gates creep away.
The ramp zooms past.
The shops run past.

Bobby Fallarino (12)
Lancasterian School

FROM A BUS WINDOW

Mum is waving from the door
The house creeps away
The trees, fence and gates
Go rushing by.

Frank Lee (12)
Lancasterian School

I'LL ALWAYS LOVE HIM

I saw him walk through the door
And then I finally saw,
When I looked in his eyes,
They sparkled like a star in the night skies,
When I saw him sitting on the other side of the room,
My heart just went *boom!*

I think I'm falling in love,
As he's as sweet as a dove,
I would try my best to fly,
If it meant we could be together until one of us die,
Every time we are apart,
It really breaks my heart.

Zoe Louise Mulvihill (12)
Newall Green High School

SPACE WOLF

Kurgen Iron Wolf, slayer of aliens,
Servant of the Emperor.

Great Wolf he was, the axe
Of Morkai was at his side

Then one day he rode to battle
His Wolf guard ready to stand and die.

At the valley end demons came.
'Forward! Forward!' cried Kurgen.

Forward the Grey Hunters, forward the Blood Claws,
into the Fire of Chaos charged the six hundred.

Kurgen felled many, before succumbing to a demon's might.
And years later the dreadnoughts say, 'The mighty Kurgen
                                                      fell that day!'

And when the Wolf Brothers fight they yell and shout,
'Forward, for Kurgen and Russ!'

Stephen Collins (12)
Newall Green High School

CIRCLE OF FATE!

Do you want to see my treasure?
Follow me, it will be my pleasure.
Through the trees and across the lake,
this will be a long journey for you to make.
Through the maze of grand, bushy trees,
feel the shimmer of a sharp, cool breeze.
Through the cave and swim to shore,
don't give up yet, there's much, much more.
Take a minute to get your breath,
if you are not determined you shall meet your death.
Tackle the lion and outwit the bear,
keep going, it's a double dare.
Follow the path that leads the way,
look at the sky, it's turning grey.
Just creep under that tree,
peer through the branch, what do you see?
An empty chest that's not right,
oh, see the moon, it's nearly night.
24, 19, 13, 9,
you shall have the fate that once was mine.
Look, it's happened, there's a ring,
do you wonder what fortune it will bring?
It shall bring power that only you can use,
do what you will with it but do not abuse.
For if you are selfish and greedy inside,
you shall have to mend your ways and
                              swallow your pride.

Vanessa Atherton (14)
Newall Green High School

DO I HAVE TO?

'I think I have a disease, Mum
Or maybe just the flu
I don't feel well, Mum
And the school could catch it too!'

'Now stop telling lies
Get up out of bed
Get dressed and washed, behave yourself
And do just like I said.'

'I think it's a holiday, Mum
A teacher training day
And because I have the flu, Mum
I might lose my way.'

'Now stop telling lies
Get up out of bed
Get dressed and washed, behave yourself
And do just like I said.'

'I think I haven't done my homework, Mum
My maths was due today
The library isn't open, Mum,
So I can't do it at play.'

'Now stop telling lies
Get up out of bed
Get dressed and washed, behave yourself
And do just like I said.'

Lucy Gill (12)
Newall Green High School

THE PUNISHMENT

I think it's fair to say
to get through the day
it's hard not to get a . . .
Detention

When at school
if you ignore the rules . . .
Detention

If you smoke
or have a joke . . .
Detention

Forget your kit
or homework missed . . .
Detention

Messing around
on the school ground . . .
Detention

I think it's fair to say
to get through the day
it's hard not to get a . . .
Detention.

Matthew Campbell (12)
Newall Green High School

MUD!

I think that mud is great
I play in it until it's late
I love to make big mud pies
And throw them into people's eyes.

I'm a mess, what will Mum say?
'No more playing in the mud today,'
So I lie down in a big heap
And hopefully I'll go to sleep.

Matthew Neild (12)
Newall Green High School

GOING ON HOLIDAY

Finally we are going
We are going away.
Over the sea we fly
Looking below at the waves.

Bump onto the floor
The plane finally came in,
Everybody was excited
And everything went in the bin.

We got up early
And out we went
Off to all the theme parks
The wheelchair we got was a rent.

It was time to go now
And off we went home.
We knew we had some good times
Including ringing home on the phone.

Bump onto the floorground
The plane finally came in.
Everybody was tired
And everything went in the bin.

Craig Rigby (12)
Newall Green High School

THE BUG 2!

I'm ill again, it isn't fair
My chest is burning but my mum doesn't care
I'm in pain, I am dying
My mum doesn't care even though I'm crying
She makes me go to school
She's really cruel
In games I couldn't run
In maths I got done
In English I couldn't write
My English teacher's really tight
She gave me a detention
For not paying any attention
In drama I couldn't act
I fell over, in fact
It was 2.20, just one hour to go
The time went really slow
I could finally go home, I walked out of the school gate,
I was out of school, it was really great
I stepped into my house and saw my mum,
                                  whom I hate.
I'll get you back, just you wait!

Daniel Boyle (12)
Newall Green High School

I'M ANGRY!

I'm angry at her
Because she thinks she's so good
My head's burning with anger
Oh I wish I could:

I wish I could kill her
I wish she would die
I wish she would stop telling
Those awful nasty lies.

I'm angry at her
Because she was supposed to be my bud
My blood's gone black with anger
Oh I wish I could:

I wish I could kill her
I wish she would die
I wish she would stop telling
Those awful nasty lies.

Natalie Chapman (13)
Newall Green High School

A TIGER'S DIARY

Monday
Made bed out of leaves and slept and slept.

Tuesday
Slept while Mother played with cubs

Wednesday
Bit zookeeper's arm, Mother and cubs
mad at me.

Thursday
Slept, ate, and drank and slept.

Friday
Mother gave birth and I slept.

Saturday
Mother's eyes were burning bright.
Vandals set the zoo alight.

Sunday
We both survived and cubs too.
We all transferred to another zoo.

Danielle Preston (12)
Newall Green High School

HALLOWE'EN

Chitter, chatter
The people have seen
Playing, laughing
The children have been
Because tonight, the night
Is Hallowe'en!

Ghosts, witches
Are everywhere
Paint and masks
With long black hair
Because tonight, the night
Is Hallowe'en!

Yes! Tonight
When midnight strikes
The witches come
To scare and fright
As tonight, the night
Is Hallowe'en!

'You can't escape!'
The witches said
As they took the children
From their beds
Because tonight, the night
Is Hallowe'en!

They contacted their parents
Via a witchy text
But we don't know
What happened next
Because tonight, the night
Is Hallowe'en!

Michelle Roscoe (12)
Newall Green High School

HIT AND RUN

I am a hit man
Hear me roar,
For I am the ruler
Of you all.

I'm a silent stalker
So be aware.
The last thing you'll see
Is my soul-piercing stare.

I get paid money
For taking your life;
May it be with gun
Or sharp-edged knife.

A cold-blooded killer
That's all I be
This is between
Only you and me.

For you're my next victim
Say your last prayer
Take your last breath
You're going to die.

When I pull this trigger
Say goodbye

For I am the hit man
Hear me roar,
For I am the ruler
Of you all.

Paul Daly (15)
Newall Green High School

BONFIRE NIGHT

Everything goes off with a sparkle
And all of the colours look like a fantastic marble
Everything goes bang and boom
And the fireworks dash and zoom!

You can smell the smoke in the air
Children and adults outside everywhere
All you can hear is snap, crackle and pop
And you don't want it to ever stop.

All of the illuminations
And all of these celebrations
All come in one night
Giving all animals a fright.

Daniel Telfer (12)
Newall Green High School

MY PARK

The park near my house was really a state,
It was a private place for animals to mate.
The council men had to clean it up,
This one time they found a savaged pup.
It had swings, which were rusted all over,
On the field, kids surrounded a burnt-out Nova.
The grass on the field had grown really high,
So much pooh, reminded me of a pigsty.
You couldn't do anything, because of the grass,
And when you came off it was stuck up your . . .

Carl Brady (14)
Newall Green High School

THE STORM

The sun shines bright every day,
but then the clouds come out,
and it goes away.

Then all of a sudden, here comes rain,
I hate rain, it's such a pain.

But then strikes lightning,
it can be very frightening.

Here comes hail,
it's sharp as a nail.

With one big bang, it all has stopped,
it was like a fizzy bottle that popped!

Nicola Fox (12)
Newall Green High School

EGGS

Eggs and chips are my favourite food.
When my mum makes it, I'm in a great mood.
Eggs and sausage is not that bad.
But egg and chips is what makes me glad.
The yoke is my favourite part.
I always eat it before I start.
I could eat eggs all day
But my mum has something to say,
'Eggs are not that good for you,
Why don't you eat my precious stew?'

Jamie Price (11)
Newall Green High School

MUSIC

Music, music
Beats all night long
Sweaty people
Begin to pong
Banging drums
And wiggling bums.

Music, music
Beats through the streets
You can feel the vibration
From the beats
People singing to
Their favourite songs
Rapidly moving
Their dancing tongues.

Music, music
And the hokey-cokey
Let's end the night
With the karaoke.

Hannah Willis (14)
Newall Green High School

DARREN H

Darren Huckerby is the best,
He's better than the rest,
And when he scores,
The crowd roars,
United is beat at last.

Leanne Petit (12)
Newall Green High School

FRIENDS

Friends are the family
We choose for ourselves.
Friends are the people we love to be around.
That cheer you up when you are down.
Friends respect the things you love
And are with you when times are tough.
But if you want to keep them this way
You have an important part to play.
Be good, be kind, be sweet,
Don't discard them for new people you meet.
Yes, friends are the family
We choose for ourselves.

So choose wisely!

Rebekah Hill (12)
Newall Green High School

SUNFLAKES

If sunflakes fell like snowflakes,
gleaming yellow and so bright,
we could build a sunman,
we could have a sunball fight,
we could watch the sunflakes,
drifting in the sky,
we could go sleighing,
in the middle of July,
through sundrifts and sunbanks,
we could ride a sunmobile,
and we could touch sunflakes,
I wonder how they'd feel!

Amany El-Sayed (12)
Newall Green High School

FOOTBALL'S A GREAT SPORT

Football's a great sport:
Once I've rested my injury
I go in hard, that's ma sort.

I like to leave them on de deck,
clutching their knees wid a broken neck.

Soon as de ball touches me feet
I look for goal, like a steam train.
Some people call me insane
When I come off the pitch with a bloodstain

'Are you alright?'
'Tisn't ma blood.'
'You'd better watch where your feet are stood.'

'I couldn't help it, me arm's in air'
On de pitch no one comes near
'Cause I'm a 'bloody' scare.

I steam down the pitch
Like a computer glitch
No way to stop me, just go for me switch

Go in wid your feet fury
Come out, I receive glory

Dis is me story
Dis is how football is a great sport
And this is my thought.

Nathan Brookes (14)
Newall Green High School

CAT THOUGHTS

I, the cat, have many mysteries,
like when all day I just climb trees.
I might tell you some of my secrets today,
let's start off with when I play.

You think I'm naughty when I dig up the yard,
I'm looking for treasure, it's fun but hard.
I also like to chase the mousy runt,
I'm not being nasty, it's called mouse hunt.

Now let's talk about the things I hate,
like when I'm waiting for my food and my owner's late.
I hate that horrid dog next door,
he rolls in the mud and drools on the floor.

Now to tell you all about me,
I'm a tabby cat, as you can see.
I have yellow eyes, as shiny as glass,
I like to look at the traffic and watch it pass.

My tail is thin with a black tip at the end,
you can only see the tip of it when I run round a bend.
My paws look like I am wearing socks,
my owner says I look like a fox.

I'm sad to say I have to go,
I hope you have really enjoyed my show.
You might see me sometime creeping through a bush,
but right now I'm sleeping, so please, just hush!

Jayne Cookson (12)
Newall Green High School

TRAMPOLINING

There I was bouncing
The best in my class
Then I fell
Right on my a**

I brushed it off
And didn't care
Until my top
Flew in the air

Boys to the left
Boys to the right
I bet they got
A real good sight

My face went red
I wanted to cry
So I ran away
To curl up and die

The moral of this tale
Is to tuck in your shirt
To save yourself from
Embarrassment and hurt.

Natalie Braddock (15)
Newall Green High School

LIFE'S INCREDIBLE

I think life's incredible
I wish we didn't have to die
Most people lie
And say they'd love to die

I think life's incredible
There's lots I'd love to do
Like go to clubs and learn to drive
That's why life's incredible.

Anthony Fox
Newall Green High School

HALLOWE'EN

I am the Queen
of Hallowe'en
I'm Minnie Mean.

I'm part of Hallowe'en
I'm Minnie Mean
With my raggy clothes.
I love to make people scream.
I'm part of Hallowe'en.

I'm part of Hallowe'en
I'm Minnie Mean
With my messy hair
I'm very, very mean
I'm part of Hallowe'en.

I cackle and crackle
Fly on my broom
I'm Minnie Mean
I'm part of Hallowe'en.

I'm the Queen
Of Hallowe'en
I'm Minnie Mean.

Terry Lee (12)
Newall Green High School

THINGS I LIKE . . .

One of the things I like the most
are boys, oh yeah, I cannot boast

And all of the things they have to say
are so funny, and sometimes gay.

Another thing I like the most
is chocolate, oh yeah, I cannot boast

But the way it tastes and the way it smells
is so nice, like pretty bluebells.

And the final thing that I like the most
is shopping, oh yeah, I cannot boast

But the way it feels when you buy new things
is just like a brilliant dream.

So this is the end of our brilliant thing
and enjoy your life because you don't know
                             what it will bring.

Kimberley Sutton & Simone Humphries (12)
Newall Green High School

MY BEST FRIEND KERRY

When you're happy
When you're merry,
Just think of my
Best friend Kerry.

She may be giddy,
She may be sad,
You never know
She could turn bad.

She could be naughty,
She could be good,
She'll always be my best bud,
That's my friend Kerry.

Caroline McGovern (12)
Newall Green High School

BONFIRE NIGHT

Finally it's 5th of November,
The night that everyone can remember.
Fireworks fly,
In the dark, dark sky,
This is the night for colour and magic.

The bonfire is ready,
The dummy is on it,
The children get ready,
The darkness is lit,
This is the night for colour and magic.

Hats and gloves are all around us,
People are trying to keep warm,
The fireworks are flying all around us,
'Stand behind!' the adults warn,
This is the night for colour and magic.

Toffee apple is the snack of the night,
Families smile as everyone watches,
The display is very bright,
The warm cat, inside he watches,
This is the night for colour and magic.

Farah Hussain (12)
Newall Green High School

CHICKENPOX AND FLU

My mum has got the chickenpox
My dad has got the flu
My little brother is playing up
And my sisters are too.

The house looks like a pigsty
My nanna is going mad
I am going out now
And I'm extremely glad.

My mum has got the chickenpox
My dad has got the flu
My little brother is playing up
And my sisters are too.

My mum is getting better
I don't know about my dad
My sisters are still playing up
But my brother, he's not as bad.

Elizabeth Nixon (12)
Newall Green High School

EXCUSES

'Miss, I didn't do my homework
My dog ate it last night
Really Miss, I couldn't
It gave me such a fright
Its teeth are like a shark's
Its growl is like a lion's
So does it matter Miss
If I could copy Ryan's?'

'Miss, I didn't come to school on time
The bus was late today
Really Miss, it was
I got kidnapped on the way.
The man was wearing a robber's mask
And a balaclava.
But who did he bump into?
Thank God it was my father!'

Chloé Brelsford (12)
Newall Green High School

TEACHERS - GOOD AND BAD

The maths teacher is nasty
The maths teacher is mean
The maths teacher is horrible
With most of her teeth green

The maths teacher hates kids
The maths teacher is fat
The maths teacher's hair is grey
And it looks like a dead rat

The English teacher is nice
The English teacher is good
The English teacher does all things
Good teachers should

The English teacher is great
The English teacher is cool
The English teacher thinks that
The maths teacher is a fool!

Natalie Grimsley (13)
Newall Green High School

HOCKEY-MAD

I am Stephen Hutchinson
I like hockey a lot
If I go too mad
I might lose the plot.

My friends don't think I'm good,
They all shout, 'You're bad. You're bad.'
I think they're the mad ones
When I win and score I will be glad.

My friends say I won't win this
If they ask me I think I just might,
At the end of a winning game
They came and said, 'You're right.'

To tell you the truth
I thought I was rubbish, but why?
At the end of the game
It was a tie.

You know what they call me?
They call me 'the taker',
I kind of like this name
Because I'm Stephen Hutchinson,
                the hockey player.

Stephen Hutchinson (12)
Newall Green High School

FOOTBALL

Football, football, is so good
football, football, in wet mud.
Kick the ball into space,
but watch it doesn't go in your face.

When the ball comes, go on a run,
and then shoot it like a gun.
The final score is one-nil
that's because we've got skill.

Jake McNicholls (12)
Newall Green High School

EVIL

I'm evil,
An assailant in league with the night,
I enjoy unnatural death
Murder, drugs, rape; moral evil.
September 11th terrorism,
Man-made evil,
I'm evil.

Evil me,
Enjoys natural disasters,
From landslides to earthquakes,
Flooding, famine, all the same,
I'm the Grim Reaper,
I enjoy taking life,
I'm evil.

The evil in me is,
Active in the day and at night,
I can metamorphesise,
To have no form,
To be both grotesque and beautiful,
The law cannot stop me or the evil in me,
I'm evil,
Cos I am the Devil.

Matthew Wilde (14)
Newall Green High School

DOLPHINS

Dolphins are the best,
They're faster than the rest.
Soft and smooth,
You should see the way they move.

They race through water like thunder and lightning,
It's not at all frightening.
They jump and dive out of the water,
Like someone professionally taught her
To swim with one would be a dream,
But to them it's an everyday thing.

Dolphins are quick,
They swim through the water, smooth and slick.

Dolphins are clever,
As cute as ever!

Megan Cole (11)
Newall Green High School

HAPPY

I'm happy,
Happy as a banana or an orange,
Or a sun in different shades of *yellow* or *orange*.
Happy as *yellow, orange* or *pink*.
Happy as a flute or clarinet.
Happy as a cat, who's just got the cream.
In fact the happiest I have ever been.

Emma Murphy (11)
Newall Green High School

I'VE GOT A DOG CALLED LUCKY

I've got a dog called Lucky,
I found her on the street
I brought her home that night
and fed her all my meat

I've got a dog called Lucky,
she's kind and gentle too
not a harmful bone in her
but she chewed my shoe.

I've got a dog called Lucky,
she sleeps all day and barks all night
I don't sleep until, 'Shut up Lucky,'
we all pray my mum to say.

I've got a dog called Lucky,
she follows me everywhere
even to the car
she loves walking far.

I've got a dog called Lucky,
she loves being with me
I know she'll never run away cos
she loves drinking all my tea.

Laura Marino (13)
Newall Green High School

BART IS THE MAN

Bart is crazy, Bart is mad,
He has been playing on his skateboard since he was a little lad.
He has a dangerous catapult, he fires it everywhere
Even at Principal Skinner in his underwear.

Laurence Wardle (11)
Newall Green High School

JEWEL
(A love poem to my rough collie, Jewel)

There they were, six bundles of fur
Huddled together without a stir
Over he came and licked my hand
This puppy, the colour of white and sand

He was the one for me, I knew
Trying to lick my hand and shoe
I've had him now for five years this year
He sometimes makes me shed a tear.

This is love from the bottom of my heart
I will love him until the day we part
His name is Jewel, he's my pet
Love is this and more I expect

Till the day he goes to the pets in the sky
I will love him forever and probably cry.

Melissa Green (13)
Newall Green High School

CHILDREN AT NIGHT

At night darkness falls
Shadows crawl across the walls,
Children lock their doors
Check under beds and on the floors.

In the street the lights come on bright
Children don't dare walk out in the night,
Out comes the moon
Casts a grey gloom.

In the morning
Children get up yawning,
Leaving behind the fright,
Until the next night . . .

Jason Whitwell (13)
Newall Green High School

SORROW

I sit here under this tree,
wondering what to do.
Is my life worth more?
Please, I'm asking you.
I wonder what I've done wrong,
to deserve this hurt and sorrow.
I feel hurt today,
and probably the same tomorrow.
I could get a rope,
and tie it to my bed.
I'd wrap it round my neck
and soon I'd be dead.
I feel so sad,
thinking about this.
I also think of my friends,
that surely I'd miss.
I look up at the sky,
and stare up into space.
At least I know,
that my heart's in the right place.
Now I know,
why I've got to live.
Because life is,
the most precious gift.

Aaron David Fairhurst (13)
Newall Green High School

SPIDERS

Monday
Running through the woods seeing what I see.

Tuesday
Heard rustling between the leaves and sticks.

Wednesday
Began to make a web then when I had finished
went down the tree.

Thursday
Found a centipede, took it to my web
then began to eat it leg after leg.

Friday
Full up and stuffed up, time for bed.

Lee Matthews (12)
Newall Green High School

MY LITTLE CAR

Stepping out of my door there sits my car,
Squinting my eyes I can see it from afar.
Just lying there on the road
Oh, I do wish it had sports mode.
Going to work it's such a long way
Chugging in my little car on the motorway.
Changing lanes to the inner section oh, I do have to go fast
But then seeing all those fast cars, they really do zoom past.
Finally reaching my destination I always have to turn and face
My little car sitting there in the same old, little space.

Roisin Cryan (12)
Newall Green High School

MY BROTHER MATTHEW

My brother Matthew
that is his name
he likes to scream
and play lots of games.
He likes to jump,
kick and scream.
When we come in
he cares for us
then by the evening
he is annoying.
He likes to laugh
and pull my hair.
He kicks the dog
then goes for the cat
but when he's asleep,
you don't hear a peep,
he looks like an angel
when he's asleep.

Victoria Ludden (13)
Newall Green High School

SMILE

I love to smile
It makes me happy
When I'm feeling down
Every time I smile I look like a
Jolly, old clown.
My cheeks start hurting after a bit,
But I keep on smiling
So it looks like the
Whole world's lit.

Lois Farrar (11)
Newall Green High School

THE BIG ONE

You queue for an hour,
And you see the tower,
When you slowly get to the top.

You see the view,
And you say to yourself,
'I knew I should have gone on something else.'

You stop at the top,
And prepare for the drop.
There's no turning back right now.

You shoot, you swivel, drop and stop.
Turn from side to side,
And jump over the bumps.
Get ready to jump high in the sky.

Now the ride has finished.
You want another go.
But your parents just say, *'No, no, no!'*

Ryan Done (13)
Newall Green High School

MONKEYS

Every day swinging from tree to tree,
Bananas are all they eat for their tea,
All day they lounge about,
Sitting, looking bored, doing nowt,
They don't have to go to school,
They just play around looking cool!

Charlotte Cordingley (11)
Newall Green High School

END MY PAIN

I don't know why they all tease me!
Is it hate or jealousy?
Inside their hearts they'll never know
Just how much it hurts me so.
I come to school, do nothing wrong,
It doesn't matter, they're just too strong.
It's not so much the physical pain,
But the names drive me insane.
I feel I'm alone, there's no one there,
My friends and family don't even care.
I cannot blame them for no one I've told,
At night I cry, my heart turns cold.
Everyone laughs as I walk through the door,
Kick! Punch! I fall to the floor.
I'm sorry but this I can take no more,
I run to my room and lock the door.
I grab my scarf, tie it to my bed,
Wrap it round my neck, I'll soon be dead.

Hannah Cummings (13)
Newall Green High School

DAVID BECKHAM

Beckham, Beckham is the best.
Better than all the rest.
He just doesn't have a rest.
He flies through the best
And can beat all the rest.

Kieran O'Hare (11)
Newall Green High School

EGG

You know it's there,
it's not in your hair
it's filled with yoke
you can always joke
taking off the shell
it can be Hell
you can buy them in Tesco
even Kwik Save
but don't put them
in the microwave,
poor little chicken
laying all night
to give them up,
it'll put up a fight.

Daniel Finlay (13)
Newall Green High School

DEATH

Death is evil, death is not kind,
Death is something that plays with your mind
You get burned or buried
You have not got a say on when you die
That horrid day
You don't know
When it's going to come
When you lose your love or Mum
Your family gathers
There is nothing to say
Oh, when you die
That very sad day!

Stephanie Downing (14)
Newall Green High School

SHOPPING

Most young ladies like to shop
and when they do they never stop.
Shopping, shopping, till they drop,
they just never seem to stop.

Shop to shop, place to place
they just can't find anything to put on their face.
They shop all day, they shop all night
I don't know how they do it
without putting up a fight.

Finally, they've stopped
and believe me, they've dropped.
You should see them on the floor,
they do look so poor.
Do you think they're tired after shopping
Monday, Tuesday, Wednesday,
Thursday Friday, the day they dropped?
Everyone's glad cos now they've stopped.

Louise Towse (12)
Newall Green High School

WIND

Wind is fast and furious and cold.
It could blow you off your feet.
As fast as a creak on the stairs.
It blows and blows and you can't escape
We run and run until we faint.

Stephanie Taylor (13)
Newall Green High School

FOOD IS GREAT

Food is great.
Food is fab.
Food is absolutely bad.

It comes in tins.
It comes in trays.
It comes in trolleys,
And in the bags.

It grows on trees.
It grows on the ground.
It grows in soil.

Food is absolutely fab!

Marcus Ely (13)
Newall Green High School

THE SWEET SHOP

It seems like the week never ends,
But finally it's Friday and I get my spends.
Two pounds for me and away I go,
Save my spends? I don't think so!
Through that door, it's a whole new world,
With chewy laces, long and swirled.
So many choices, which one to take?
Apple and syrup lollipops or a piece of carrot cake?
Bonbons, all the different flavours,
There's even the new ketchup Quavers.
Skipping home with a bag full of treats,
Don't you just love eating sweets?

Melissa Tennant (15)
Newall Green High School

QUICK, RUN!

It's one minute to midnight
The clouds break
The full moon's out
Quick, run, hide.

The witches on their brooms
Swooping black cat, hold on tight
Spells, bats' wings, frogs' legs, rats' tails,
Quick, run, hide.

The vampires are awake
Ready to suck blood
Their yearly feast.
Quick, run, hide.

The Devil's out, alive
Setting fires, burning souls
Turning good to evil,
Quick, run, hide.

Witches, a puff of smoke
Vampires, a lid shuts
Devils, a flame
They have vanished.

Peace! Silence!
    Deserted!

Rebecca Lowe (12)
Newall Green High School

WEATHER

Spring.
Cloudy,
Sunshine,
Clear.

Summer.
Sunny,
Heatwave,
Sunshine.

Autumn.
Misty showers.
Windy,
Cloudy,
Draughty,
Frosty.

Winter.
Snowing,
Raining,
Hailstoning,
Thundering,
Lightning,
Spitting,
Frosty,
Icy,
Foggy.

Tanya Suddons (12)
Newall Green High School

My Dad's Kawasaki Ninja

Green and mean
a lean machine.
It's so mean,
it will make you scream.

He rides his bike.
He looks so good
but he rides it too fast,
I don't think he should.

He drives down the road
as fast as can be,
if he saw a traffic cop,
he would have to flee.

Sometimes he'd go over
seventy miles an hour.
When he takes of his leathers,
he definitely needs a shower.

Jason Kane (13)
Newall Green High School

Winter Weather

Winter has come and summer has gone.
That grey brick wall is no more!
That white bright snow has covered the floor!
Birds have gone, gone for winter.
Only the brave stay for those long winter days!
Until that day the snow comes once again.
I'll be waiting until that day.

Simon Peak (12)
Newall Green High School

SCHOOL DAY

I go to school feeling happy and right
but there at the school gate is a fight.
I run to the front to see who is fighting.
They always do it and end up writing.

I get into class with a grin on my face
I'm late and my teacher's in disgrace.
Dinner time came, I felt lame
Then I realised I had a football game.

The end of the day is here
I have a pain in my ear
I go to the gate to meet my mate
But I've got to be home for eight.

Lucas Billingham (12)
Newall Green High School

CARS

Cars, cars, are everywhere
Cars, cars, are everywhere
There's not a place where
Cars are not
Cars, cars, are everywhere
You find them in shop
You find them on road
And also you find them in rows.
Some are cheap,
Some are dear,
Some are not even
Worth a pint of beer!

Joshua Howarth (12)
Newall Green High School

MY BROTHER JOSH

My brother Josh is a pest,
he's even worse than the rest,
Josh is his name, I say,
he really loves to play.
He has lots of friends,
I think there are four,
maybe even,
many more,
Ellis, Gemma, Georgie, Jack,
they always sit on a mat.
He's only two,
he can't tie a shoe,
his mummy is so great,
she puts him in bed for half-past eight,
his mummy then turns off the light,
then she shouts, 'Night, night!'
He cuddles up with teddies too,
his favourite one's a dog called Blue.

Laura Hampson (13)
Newall Green High School

MY BEST FRIEND EVER

My best friend
is so close to me
when we see each other,
we're meant to be,
she makes me smile,
we laugh together
cos she's my mum
and my best friend ever.

Holly Candlin (12)
Newall Green High School

DRUGS AND ALCOHOL

Drugs are bad
Alcohol is so sad
If you take them or drink them you are mad.
You might do it for a buzz
You might do it for fun
It might be a laugh
Or it might be a joke,
But you are the one who wouldn't
                be able to drive the boat.
Drugs are bad
Alcohol is so sad
You think they are cool
You might do it to escape reality
You might get addicted to them.

Selina Farrington (13)
Newall Green High School

POEM OF LOVE

Love is forever
never to part
because you will always
be in my heart.
I love you
you love me
always and forever
we will be.
You hug me
I hug you
that's why
I love you.

Leanne Price (12)
Newall Green High School

MY LOVE

He was my love, he was my charm
but there was a secret behind those hazel eyes.
Days went by, sometimes I even cried
Was it me or something else?
I stared out the window into the sky
He passed by with a sigh
I passed a note to share my emotion
He said, 'Pass it back, it's another silly love potion.'
I asked his friend was there something wrong.
He said, 'I don't know' and carried on singing a song.
I built up my courage to go and speak to him.
He smiled so I said to him.
'I want you forever.'
He exclaimed, 'You'll be my soulmate for all eternity.'

Jennifer Duff (14)
Newall Green High School

MY FAT BROTHER

My brother is a brat
He looks like a rat
He went to the shops
Bought some chops
He climbed a mountain
That spat out a fountain
That spat out money
Which he kept counting
He licked up peas
And sliced up bees.
So there we go,
That's how my brother got
                      fat!

Anthony Law (11)
Newall Green High School

THE DAY OF THE MATCH

I woke up one morning to the day of the match
City and United, they were no match.
I threw on my T-shirt, trousers and boots,
I could hear the crowds shouting, oh, it's two-nil.

We were off in the car, my shirt so light blue
People were walking all dressed in blue.

I saw Maine Road as I was coming up in the car
All the fans entering of course, going straight to the bar.

I entered the ground with a leap and a cheer
I looked for my seat with some crisps and a beer.

The players ran out, the crowd going nuts.
Me going ballistic and throwing peanuts.

They were running like mad till their hearts were content
Oh, it's Wanchope to make it two-nil.

Five minutes left and it's only 2-1,
But can Huckerby make it to make it 3-1? *Yeah!*

The end of the match, we won 3-1,
We left in the cold and me with a numb bum.

Daniel Holt (11)
Newall Green High School

THE SNOWMAN

Come in the garden
And play in the snow
A snowman we'll make
See how quickly he'll grow!

Give him a hat, stick and pipe
Make him look gay
It's such a fine game
On a cold winter's night.

Jessica Jarratt (12)
Newall Green High School

MOB RULES

There is a mob in Central Manchester,
The leader is a guy called Big Hester.
They'd go around causing riots,
Stabbing people who were on diets.
No gang could match their evil ways,
Not even the notorious Krays.
They went over to Wythenshawe Park,
Shooting people lost in the dark.
Their victims were normal and innocent,
But not according to Mr Vincent.
They drove around in black coupés,
Blowing off old men's toupees.
One victim, Old Man Jake,
They decided to give his neck a break.
They described themselves as the ultimate villains.
They went round and shot the Dillans.
They dealt with drugs and all that stuff,
But when the going got tough, they turned rough.
In the end it came to a stop,
All because of a lucky cop.
But now they serve behind bars,
Beaten up, full of scars.

      Oh well, it's your own fault!

Mark Harrop (14)
Newall Green High School

THUNDERSTORM

As I walked through the moody moor
The wind rushed at my knees.
My legs withered with fear.
The dark, gloomy hairs
on my back stood up at a halt.
I started to run -
My face was as red as a beetroot
on a boiling hot summer's day.

As the thunderstorm started
I smelt fresh sea-salted air.
I knew it all started
Because of Him
Up there.

James Davenport (14)
Newall Green High School

FRIENDSHIP

F or being there for each other
R ight or wrong, always forgive
I   'm there for my friends.
E verlasting friendship
N ever give up on your friends
D on't leave your friends out.
S ay sorry if you hurt them
H elp them with their problems.
I   have friends, you have friends.
P eople love to have friends.

Nicola Hewitt (12)
Newall Green High School

SUMMER WEATHER

The sun glazed on Monday morning,
but I was so sleepy I felt like yawning,

Tuesday's sun was brighter than ever,
there had never been such sunny weather.

On Wednesday, bursts of cloud were breaking
through on our street. It was a nice change
from that boiling heat.

On Thursday, the clouds had gone,
so the weather was number one.

Friday's sun was clearer than glass
so we all sat out on the grass.

Saturday's sun was bluer than the sea,
so that is all I could see.

Sunday's sun went down and down
so that was the end of our sunny town.

Laura Carbert (14)
Newall Green High School

IS IT LOVE OR INFATUATION?

Sometimes I think will I ever fall in love or not,
I really like this guy but I don't know if it's love or not.
He always says, 'I love you,' but how do I know whether it is
 true or not,
Please, someone, help me because I don't know what to do.
He always smiles and winks at me.
He always says, 'Do you want to come to my house for tea?'

Amy Herbert (12)
Newall Green High School

MANCHESTER CITY

Manchester City are the best
Manchester City can take on any test
Manchester United are so pooh
Manchester United need the loo.

Manchester City are the best
Manchester City are better than the rest
Manchester United are so lame
Manchester United won't play the game.

Manchester City can take a test
Manchester City are just the best
Manchester United are a piece of trash
Manchester United always crash.

Manchester City are the best
Manchester City can beat the rest.

So just face it!

Lee McGuinness (12)
Newall Green High School

BUNNIES

Bunnies are funny
Bunnies are bonny
Bunnies are funny
Like Jim Dunny
Bunnies are pink
Bunnies are red
A colour you can't get
    out of your head
Until you go to bed.

Wayne Hobbs (11)
Newall Green High School

THE MOUSE IN MY HOUSE

There is a mouse
In my house.
My cat came along
Thought the mouse was strong.
Scared was the cat
And hid under the mat.
The mouse was on the floor,
Next to the door
And got a shock,
From the knock.
It is a midge,
Compared to the fridge.
It used a cup,
To get up.
When he had all the cheese,
He came down and died of fleas.

Michael Crosse (11)
Newall Green High School

I'M GRUMPY

I mumble
Under
My
Breath
Feel my temper
Like a burning flame
I'm a storm
A mean hyena
A sneaky snake
I'm grumpy
So move!

Adam Taylor (11)
Newall Green High School

SECRETS

I have a secret nobody knows
I might tell my friend

Shhh . . . shhh . . .

She doesn't even know yet
She'll tell her friends I bet

Well, her mind is like something flying by
I don't know why

I don't know what to do
Should I tell her . . .
Or be a durr?

But I need someone to know
Or I think I'm going to blow

Shhh . . . shhh . . .

Natalie Simpson (13)
Newall Green High School

DOLPHINS

Sleek and slender
they swim through the sea
they are happy every day
just like me.

They swim through the
sea every day, being happy
as I pray.

Aimee Benn (11)
Newall Green High School

MOVE YOUR FEET TO THE BULLY BEAT

Bullies give you verbal
bullies give you stress
bullies make you feel down, devastated and depressed.
It makes you scared and stressed out,
makes you want to scream and shout
that's not what life's about.
Let's get together and sort it out.

I want to live my life, just leave me be
I don't want to be bullied, can't you see?
So why, why, why do they pick on me?
Why, why, why, do they pick on me?

Heather Anderson (14)
Newall Green High School

HAPPY

As happy as a bird in the sky,
As happy as a big cherry pie,
As happy as a loud beeping horn,
As happy as a bright green lawn,
As happy as a nice juicy peach,
As happy as the hot sandy beach
As happy as the shiny rainbow,
As happy as the sound of a piano,
As happy as luminous pink,
As happy as a silver shining sink,
As happy as a waggling hog's tail,
As happy as a big wet whale.

Rochelle Williams (14)
Newall Green High School

MY SECRET

I have the biggest secret
I'll never ever tell
But it gets me very stressed
So I think I'm gonna yell.

I could have told my friend
I start to wish I had
Maybe if I did that
I might not be so mad.

When I'm in my bedroom
I lie down on my bed
Then I start to scream because
That secret's in my head.

I go in school on Monday
He's stood right over there
My knees have gone like jelly
But I just stand and stare.

Suddenly he looks at me
Everything starts to rush
I think that I've gone crazy
I think I have a crush.

Then he walks right over
My heart begins to pound
Then he says hello to me
But I can't make a sound.

He starts to walk away from me
So I just shout out, 'Hi!'
But then he just goes silent
And then he says goodbye.

I feel so relieved
Now that my secret's out
It makes me feel better
Because I don't have to shout.

Jenny Bruton
Newall Green High School

MISS, I CAN'T WRITE

'Miss, I can't write'
'Why?'
'Well at dinner time
I was playing football
and I was in net
I did a classy save
but the up-fronter
hit the ball hard
and the ball whacked
against my hands and
knocked off my fingers
but they wriggled away
like little worms.
They went through the
Astro Turf fence and I got up
and they were miles ahead of me
So now I am here in literacy
bored, and my fingers are
out there . . .
They could be anywhere!

Robert Miller (11)
Newall Green High School

WHILE WE WERE ASLEEP

Sunday morning at quarter to three,
I heard a noise, what could it be?
Was it my mum? Was it my dad?
I had to find out, it was driving me mad.

I jumped out of my bed and slowly crept,
Came to the stairs and quietly stepped,
Then I froze, I heard it again,
Was it a stranger or was it the rain?
I ran to the kitchen and opened the door,
My favourite uncle lay on the floor,
I tried to revive him, I cradled his head,
All this was in vain, my uncle was dead.
I looked at his face, a white ghostly stare,
Who could have done this? Who couldn't care?
I shouted my mum and started to weep,
What maniac did this while we were asleep?

Stephanie Green (13)
Newall Green High School

THE SUN

The sun makes us all warm inside
Like you're sliding down the slide
How you make me feel
And the way you make me deal.

The sun

The way you make me hurt
Like the way I always flirt
And the way you help me see
As long as it doesn't hurt me.

Dale Davies (12)
Newall Green High School

THE DARK SIDE (THIS IS WAR)

The skeleton bones rise
The vampires awake
The goblins have gone away
The orcs are charging their weapons

The crossbows get scared
The spears and swords go down
The leaders don't know what to do
The ground starts shaking
The Dark Side is coming
The Empire is getting ready.

The crossbows are firing
The orcs are dying
The swords slashing
The horses are falling
The ground is tumbling
Hearing thunder
Seeing lightning

The war is over
The sound is silenced
Everyone's dead - bodies blowing away
The Dark Side has victory
The Empire falls quickly
The Dark Side will live forever!

Wade Loose (13)
Newall Green High School

DRUGS AND ALCOHOL!

Alcohol is bad
drugs are sad.
They just kill
so write your will
   so!
Alcohol is bad
drugs are sad.
If you take them
it's a mistake
   so!
Take a break
don't make a mistake
So write your will
'cause they kill
   so!
Another month,
another year,
another smile,
another tear,
another winter,
a summer too,
but there will never be
another you
if you take a drug
or a pill.

Stephanie Brennan (13)
Newall Green High School

THE THEATRE OF WAR

I cannot believe I've been dragged into the war,
Why me? Whatever for?

Tomorrow we are off to fight.
'Don't worry,' Corporal said, 'war doesn't bite.'

I heard that a soldier ran away, he was called Howard
The Corporal gunned him down and labelled him a coward.

There was an explosion close to the base, it was quite a blast.
I can't help feeling like I'm in a theatre, and I'm part of the cast

                In the theatre of war!

Kelly Jones (14)
Newall Green High School

DREAMS

My dreams always come true
My family says I lie to you

But I don't know why they say it to me

You lie, you lie, that's all you do
You lie to me, that's all you do.

You say you want to play with me
But you run away from me
You found one pence but said to me it was a quid,
You lie, you lie
That's all you do, you lie to me that's all you do.

Rebecca McWhirter (12)
Newall Green High School

THE CHOCOLATE

The ring of the bell on the factory door
The spill of milk on the factory floor
The pour of milk into the mix
Us in the cold with a giant whisk

I am completed. I start to take shape
The wrapper is sealed, like a crimson-red cape
The conveyor belt starts, with a lot more
Into the crate there - and out through the door.

The watching and waiting - naught but to stare
The engine starts as if I should care
My friends have departed, to other shops, five
My stop is here now, and now I arrive.

I stare into space, just like before
Could this be the one, as he comes through the door
His arm reaches to grab me, finally the day
He picks me up and then goes to pay.

And now it is time, it's nearly the end
I'll see you again someday, my friend
He starts to undress me, the wrapper comes off
I'll see you again someday, my . . .

Scoff!

Kevin Long (12)
Newall Green High School

FIRST DATE

At the club when I saw you standing there,
With your big blue eyes and your curly, long blonde hair,
I knew it was love - of that I had no doubt
I knew it was love -I had to ask you out

On our very first date you swept me off my feet,
You looked up at me - your smile was cool and sweet.
I knew it was love - I had to write this song
I knew it was love - why did it all go wrong?

John Gaynor (12)
Newall Green High School

DREAMLAND

When I go to bed and start to sleep
Close my eyes, I'm in dreamland deep
Nothing can wake me, not a loud beep
No waking up, no counting sheep.

In dreamland everything is free
No credit cards, no large fee
Lots of company, not just me
No loneliness when eating tea.

Non-stop go-kart
Pub games, even darts
Footy gamcs, Leeds vs Hearts
Fighting martial arts

McDonald's, yum! yum!
No tests, no one's dumb
People singing, hum! Hum!
World's best parents, Dad and Mum.

Oh no, start to wake
Mum gets up, beds to make
Time to stretch, time to ache
School time - for goodness sake.

Sam Dunbar (12)
Newall Green High School

THE NIGHTMARE GHOST

He glared at me with glowing, red eyes,
My blood ran cold, I caught a shiver
And goosebumps took over my thighs.

>I died that night,
>because of fright,
>beware of the Nightmare Ghost!

As his chill settled in, the fire exhaled
its last breath of smoke and he pounced
like a tiger and wouldn't let go,
I hoped for freedom but he wouldn't let go.

>I died that night,
>because of fright,
>beware of the Nightmare Ghost.

He caught me in my room,
he ringed me with fire and began his doom,
I hoped for death or cold rain,
then I died, in excruciating pain.

>I died that night,
>because of fright,
>beware of the Nightmare Ghost.

Sam Middleton (11)
Newall Green High School

DONALD AND HIS DREAM

Donald is still asleep in his bed
A lovely dream floats in his head.
As you can see, it is a chocolate cake,
                            as big as he.

It looks tasty, it looks sweet
What a lovely thing to eat
But when he tries to bite the cake
He suddenly becomes wide awake.

Katie Lehane (12)
Newall Green High School

FRIENDS FOREVER

My best friend is Jodie,
She's really smart and funny.
She doesn't eat a lot,
But her favourite food is honey
We will be friends forever,
Just us two alone.
But when we ignore Colleen,
She has a little moan.
My best friend is Jodie,
She's really smart and funny.
She doesn't eat a lot,
But her favourite food is honey.
We will be friends forever,
We will never grow apart.
I love my best friend, Jodie,
With all my heart.
My best friend is Jodie,
She's really smart and funny.
She doesn't eat a lot,
But her favourite food is honey
We will be friends forever,
Until our dying day,
We will have a double wedding,
And get married in May.

Rio Walker (12)
Newall Green High School

THE INNOCENT CHILD

Was she scared or just unsure?
The look on her face I couldn't ignore!

What was she facing there at home,
Was she feeling so sad and alone?

One day she was there and the next she was gone.
I asked myself, what was going on.

I never really knew her but just enough
to realise that things were getting tough.

One day, cut, the next, all bruised
I'm sorry to say she was getting abused!

I heard a bang and went to see
Her body was hanging in front of me.

This girl was gentle, innocent too,
But she wasn't able to see things through.

Megan Miller (13)
Newall Green High School

THE BEAT FOR THE MUSIC

The music is so loud
My heart beats to the sound
While my legs dance around
And my toes twitch to the sound.

I lie in bed with my head up high
While I listen to my music and cry, cry, cry.

When I wake up in the morning I growl
like my dog eating a mashed-up cake.

Brent Macauley (11)
Newall Green High School

You And I

If a laugh is a child,
What is a cry?

If an angel is Heaven,
What is Hell?

Must we die
Or must we survive?

Open the gate,
Thou shall not hate.

Shine our light because
The world is black and white.

All I want is to join you
Together forever,
        You and I.

Daniel Williams (14)
Newall Green High School

School

Come to school, it is cool
If you don't, you'll be a fool,
There's lots to do like maths,
English, drama and dance too.
If you like those things you'll give it a chance.
People say that school is boring
But how will they know if they're always drawing?
They never listen to what a teacher says,
They just sit and talk and mess around and play.
One day, they will be the ones who have to pay.

Jenny Day (14)
Newall Green High School

ENGLAND

England, not Poland,
we're the best,
that beat the rest,
so give us a test,
but no team can beat the best,
because we're the team that comes
                      from the north-west.

Craig Thompson (13)
Newall Green High School

STRANGE THINGS

I'm as thin as a rake,
As long as a snake,
I can creep under the door,
I'm very sure when I meet Mr Snail
He'll get caught in the hail
Because he is so
                      slow!

Jessica Mulvey (11)
Newall Green High School

COLOURS

Blue is like the moonlit sky
Green is like the trees passing by
Yellow is like the sun in the sky
Just look at all those colours passing by.

Aiden Billingham & Kayleigh (13)
Newall Green High School

STOCKPORT COUNTY FC

Stockport County is the club for me
I like their cheap cups of tea.

My best player is Ali Gibb
he dribbles like he needs a bib

He runs down the wing so fast
we've seen it all in the past.

Rob Clare's at the back,
Luke Beckett is the attack.

Jon Daly scores again
the other team is in pain.

Petri Helin's still in a cast
Aaron Lescott is so fast

The game against Wigan we will win
and throw Division Two in the bin.

So come down to Edgely Park
where the fans shout and bark.

James O'Brien (13)
Newall Green High School

THE MOON

The moon is purple
the moon is pink
when you look at it
you start to think
Is it black? Is it blue?
I don't know
I leave it up to you.

Alana Oven (13)
Newall Green High School

PLAYERS

Ryan Giggs has loads of goals
Japp Stam takes vision pills
Barthez has a great hand, and
David Beckham is worth one grand
Roy Keane has fair hair
He always likes to stand and stare
Paul Scholes digs holes and
Diego Forlan can't score a goal.

Aaron Holmes (12)
Newall Green High School

WONDERFUL

I think you are so wonderful
Your love you always share
And when it's comes to Christmas
It shows you really care.
You make it all so special
With everything you do
So for this Christmas
I send my love to you.

Cheryl Kane (12)
Newall Green High School

OLD MAN

I cannot speak
I cannot eat
I cannot drink
I cannot sleep
I cannot hear
I may as well
Disappear.

Every day I don't go out
I dream of visitors
But there's a doubt
I hope for laughter
I hope for joy
I'm like an old
Forgotten toy.

Lewis Herbert (11)
Newall Green High School

THE SUN

A giant ball of fire,
forever moving round,
millions and millions of miles,
high above the ground,
floating round in space,
like a ball does in the sea,
shining down its rays,
shining them on me.

Nathan Gilbert (13)
Newall Green High School

TIGER, TIGER

I am speed,
I'm made for speed.
I have lots and lots of stripes.
I dream of having everything I like.
My sneaky hobby is chasing and eating my prey.

Warren Capper (11)
Newall Green High School

MUSIC

I listen to my music day after day,
My brothers and sisters even start to sway.

It sways into the distance, so everyone can hear,
I hear my mate's music, it is very near.

My music is very important to me,
It's more important than going to the sea.

I get embarrassed by the music I listen to
Thank God no one can hear, I thought, *phew!*

It's teatime now and I've got to go,
But stay tuned now, I'm only below.

Sara Eastwood (14)
Newall Green High School

I'M HAPPY

I'm happy as a butterfly
I feel like I could float
When I'm sailing far away in my little boat.

I got stuck in a tree
I flew right out
I stood up to shout, 'I'm a butterfly.'

Then the birds started chirping,
'See the cool butterfly'
And the butterfly flew into the blue, blue sky.

Robert James Bates (11)
Newall Green High School

MY NIECE KERRIS

My niece Kerris is nasty and mean
She bites, she scratches, she kicks and screams
Her birthday was on Wednesday
She has just turned two
When she walks through the door she says, 'Love you.'

When she comes to visit
She plays with our cat
She soon gets bored
Then ignores our poor old pussy cat.

When it's hot and sunny
She wears her flowery hat
When she takes it off
She screeches like a rat.

When she stays the night
She and her grandad fight
When she stays in my bed
She cuddles her teddy, Fred.

Leanne Berry (13)
Newall Green High School

SNAILS, SNAILS

Snails, snails, aren't very fast, but
Snails snails come from the past
Snails, snails leave a slimy trail
Snails, snails are very slow they still go, go go!
Snails, snails are my friends,
Snails, snails, please never end
Snails, snails, get places, but
Snails, snails, don't show their faces.

Jamie Morris (11)
Newall Green High School

I Wish

I wish I was a bird
So I could fly up in the sky,
I wish I was a rabbit,
So I could jump very high,
I wish I was a mouse,
Scurrying across the floor,
I wish I was a toddler,
Screaming, 'More, more, more.'
I wish I was a deer,
Walking across the grass,
I wish I was a donkey
Or in other words, an ass,
I wish I was a monkey
Swinging from tree to tree.
But I'm not any of these
Because I'm me!
I wish I was a piece of string
With two different ends,
But really, I'm glad I'm me
With all my different friends.

Karen Burt (13)
Newall Green High School

A Teenage Life

Puberty and drugs are not the best things in life,
they always seem to ruin your life.
It's only the ones who never take the drugs
who are the smartest of them all.
But that's okay, life is sweet.
Make the most of it and make sure,
puberty and drugs never ruin your life forever.

Sarah Walker (13)
Newall Green High School

THAT BOY

The boy who sits next to me is so annoying,
everything he talks about is so boring.

He sits on his chair and leans right back,
some day I wish the chair would crack!

He robs people's pencil cases to make them feel small,
and as they walk past, he trips them up and makes them fall.

He shouts out loud while he's in class,
'Miss, Miss, I need the toilet pass!'

He tries to push in the dinner line,
when someone says, 'Don't push,'
he says, 'God, it's not a crime.'

It's twenty past three, it's time to go home,
what will happen tomorrow?
We just don't know.

Nichola Parry (12) & Shadelle Logan (13)
Newall Green High School

MY TRIP TO WALES

I was in my dad's new car,
and Wales was too far.
I was going to see my gran
but I saw my Aunty Ann.
My dad was going fast
but it looked like he was in last
At last we got there
but where was the fair?

Dean Hardie (13)
Newall Green High School

SHE'LL ALWAYS BE MY SPECIAL ONE

I love you, I love you,
I really, really do.
All that gossip about you
It's nothing more but lies.

Why are you just lying there?
What's wrong with you?
Are you hurt?
I love you, I love you
I really, really do.

What's wrong with you?
What's wrong with you?
Come on, talk to me!
Say something!

'Hello! Hello!'
'It's alright
She's not in pain anymore'
'She's gone, Mum, hasn't she?'
'Yes, Love, she's no longer on this Earth.'

Anna Hoy (12)
Newall Green High School

CHOCOLATE

Chocolate is the thing to eat,
you sit down or walk and you're lifted off your feet.
The taste, the smell, it so delightful,
you still can't get a real mouthful,
but still it's only 30p,
but it's still the best thing for me.

Rachel Molloy
Newall Green High School

FRIENDS

My friends are sometimes nice,
we just hang around.
My friends are sometimes nice,
sometimes I think we're sound.
But when they get nasty
they start to call me names.
When they get nasty
they drive me insane.

Are we really friends?
I don't know.
Are we really friends?
I hope so.

Louise Parkes
Newall Green High School

FOOTBALL

Football is a great desire,
kick the ball and send it higher.
If the ball scores a goal,
kick it straight to Ashley Cole.
David Seaman saves a shot
while teammates running, getting hot.
Nicky Butt tries to score but ends up
falling on the floor.
The crowd goes wild for the England team
every English person's dream.

Jodie Armstrong (11)
Newall Green High School

WINTER

Winter is finally here
leaves falling, wind blowing,
Jack Frost comes out to play
icing the road with his icy toes.
No more is it warm,
no more will children come out, to play,
just stay indoors watching the TV
Snowflakes fall, the weather is grey
Wrap up warm, hat, gloves, scarf,
don't want to get cold.
Walk outside, too, too cold,
nose goes red, cheeks go rose.
Walk inside, my glasses steam up once again.
Next time I'll go out again is when
the sunny sun comes again!

Ashley Nunn (14)
Newall Green High School

YOU

You're far away
but close to me
I feel the breeze
flow straight past me.

The clock strikes one
and you've only just gone.

For me and you
the ride's just begun.

Rachael Taylor (12)
Newall Green High School

THE BOOGLE BOO

In the land of the Boogle Boo
there are cats and rats and people too.
They comb their hair and brush their teeth
like worms trying to get to sleep.

In the land of the Boogle Boo
they eat ice cream and chocolate too.
It's so much fun in the land of the Boogle Boo
that's the place for me and you.
So hurry up, the train leaves at one
so grab my hand and jump upon.

Leigh Townsend (12)
Newall Green High School

CLOUDS

Clouds are fluffy
Clouds are grey
Clouds are grey on a very dull day

When clouds are grey the rain is calling
When it's grey it can be very boring

When I go outside it can be quite dark
The shape of the clouds could be a shark.

When the clouds are fluffy
It can be quite sunny.

Rosie Joanne Edwards (12)
Newall Green High School

I Am In My Room

I am in my room all alone,
Go to sleep, I just can't do.
Hear the wind sway across the floor
Hear the raindrops on the outside door.

Lightning shoots across my window,
Shadows move all over my walls.
The downstairs door is flying open
But go downstairs, I wouldn't dare.

The door slams shut, they run upstairs
I cuddle to my teddy
Hoping it's not a grizzly bear.

Sarah Barclay (11)
Newall Green High School

The Weather

I love it when it's sunny
because I can play with my bunny

I hate it when it's raining
because everyone's complaining

I hate it when it's cold
because you won't be told

I love it when it's snowing
because you look like you're glowing

    and that is the weather!

Jacqueline Smith (12)
Newall Green High School

WAR

Bang! Bang!
The trigger's pulled,
The bullet's out,
John shouts,
Why me,
What did I do?
I got my knife
And ran at you,
You pulled your gun
And pinned me down,
You pulled the trigger
And watched me drown
In a pool of blood,
I started to cry,
What have I done?
I don't know why,
He's wounded there
On the floor,
All alone,
This is war!

Aston Hughes (13)
Newall Green High School

CAMEL

To have to be a camel

It is like, in a way, being a moving van going along the motorway
                                                       owned . . .
by these huge nostrils that close when they hit the sand,
and colossal broad feet which plod along.

What can you know of me, this warm, cosy lounger in the desert?

Danielle Palin (12)
Newall Green High School

THEATRE OF DREAMS

Banana kicker Beckham enters,
The red sea roars,
Left-footed cheetah races on,
The green carpet of dreams awaits,
Big hand Barthez leaps on,
The United express comes racing out
And the wall of noise cannot stop speeding towards you.

As Nistelrooy releases the trigger,
The cannonball flies in the net,
The red mists descends,
Keane, the lion, bites the ref.

The curtain comes down on another game
And the dream lives on to rise again.

Sam Morris (12)
Newall Green High School

FOOTBALL

Football is cool
Football is cruel

In the net is very cold
Cold smoke
From the mouth -
Freezing weather.

David Burns (13)
Newall Green High School

MUM

'Mum' there's that word again.
Mum, I love you more and more
She's the one that I adore
We share the ups and downs
The smiles and the frowns
Then there come the words
'No' and 'yes'
You take a guess!

We may have the good days and the bad days
Even though there's 'waheys'
We will be together forever.

Racheal McCoy (12)
Newall Green High School

HORSE

I am lightning
Wild and free
Speeding through the field is me

In the field I hear a cry
Over the lightning is
Where I'll die.

Now in Hell I will lie
Dreaming of my journey
In the sky.

Hannah Rimmington (12)
Newall Green High School

LAST FEW DAYS OF PRIMARY SCHOOL

The last few days of primary school
Easy day learning a song for assembly
Friends going to different schools
Laughter turns to tears
Tears to goodbyes
Hugging
Swapping phone numbers
First day of high school - homework
One teacher turns to six
Bus rides
Season change.

Matthew Taylor (13)
Newall Green High School

THE OLD SCHOOL

When I walk in . . .
Dead wasps on windows
Dust on doors
Rust on the roof
Cobwebs in the corners.

The school lies empty.
I walk through the old corridor
Hear laughter
Of children long gone.

Daniel Miller (14)
Newall Green High School

SUMMER TO WINTER

Summer's here,
nearly gone,
please don't leave,
I want to play.
Too late . . .
it's gone.

Winter's here,
it's blistery cold,
the snow is pounding down,
hard on my numb face,
it's taken ages . . .
well, so it seems,
I sit in front of the fire,
hurry up winter,
please go.

Jordan Harrison (11)
Newall Green High School

I CANNOT GO TO SCHOOL TODAY

I cannot go to school today
I lost my bag when I picked my sister up
I cannot go to school today
I broke my leg when I was running
I cannot go to school today
My head fell off when someone hit my neck
I cannot go to school today
Because I can't be bothered.

Lee Stevenson (11)
Newall Green High School

SOME PEOPLE...

Some people say hello
Some people play the cello
Some people talk on the telephone
Some people play the saxophone

Some people watch a different channel
Some people play the piano
Some people hang around the bar
Some people play the guitar

Some people answer a sum
Some people play a drum
Some people fish for carp
Some people play the harp.

Bradley Thomas
Newall Green High School

COMING TO SCHOOL

I love coming to school on sunny mornings
The day begins to dawn
Cock-a-doodle-doo, the horn goes
Coming to school, working
I sometimes start shirking
I hate my maths
When I go home I have a bath
I love the minute
When our freedom comes
And that is at 3.20.

Rebecca Wovenden (11)
Newall Green High School

THE BIRD

Once I saw a bird
The bird saw me
We flew around for hours on end
Then we went for tea.

We tidied up our place
Then we watched TV
We both went to bed,
That little bird and me.

In the morning we had breakfast
Then we went to play out.
We played out till 1 o'clock
Then we went to Scouts.

We had fun all weekend
I wished it would never end
Since the time I saw that bird
We have been best friends.

Sam Thomas (11)
Newall Green High School

WHY HAVEN'T I DONE MY HOMEWORK?

I was doing my homework when . . .
an alien came
and abducted it
he mistook it for
a toilet roll
I said to myself,
'This is so unfair!'

Craig Bell (12)
Newall Green High School

LEE EVANS

Lee Evans is very funny
he's got ears like a bunny
he's always live on TV
as I watch him, I eat my veggies.

His shows are so good
I wish I could
step into his shoes
and be on the news.

I'll be really funny
kind of like Bugs Bunny
then I'll change back
to my normal kind of act.

Aaron Creighton (11)
Newall Green High School

SCIENCE

I started science when I was eight
It's a subject I'll never hate.
Doing science three times a week
Sometimes I feel a bit of a geek.
Doing science with Miss Ross
Well, of course, she is the boss.
Doing science till Year 11
Then of course I'll be in Heaven.

Tiffany Connor (11)
Newall Green High School

WHAT TO WEAR

Walking through the living room,
Walking up the stairs,
Walking round the bedroom
Wondering what to wear.
It's cold outside, but it's warm in work.
Walking round the bedroom
Wondering what to wear.
Looking through the closet,
Picking out an outfit.
It's like pic 'n' mix, why can't this be fixed?
Half an hour later, everything is fixed.
Looking in the mirror, it's a perfect fit.

Rea Holly Hickman (14)
Newall Green High School

I CANNOT GO TO SCHOOL TODAY

I cannot go to school today
because I feel dizzy and I have a temperature

I cannot go to school today
because I have got tummy pains
and Miss will not let me go to the toilet.

I cannot go to school today
I'm allergic to ink, bells and other pupils.

I cannot go to school to day
because, because, just because . . .

Aaron Lyons (11)
Newall Green High School

I Am A Shark

I am speed
Raging through the waters,
I am the colour of deep, dark blue,
Scared of nothing,
With my snappy sharp teeth,
The sea is very peaceful and quiet,
I dream of having the sea to myself.

Laura Molloy (11)
Newall Green High School

Sea Horses

When sea horses mate they make a heart shape.
Sea horses look like they have big noses and mouths.
They also have a long, curly tail.
They live at the bottom of the ocean -
Sea horses hate being put in Sea Life Centres.
They eat seaweed and fish.

Chelsea Agoglia (12)
Newall Green High School

Panda

There was an man from Canada
Who bought a panda
He put it in pans
Then sold it in cans
That silly man from Canada.

Darren Horsfield-Eaves (12)
Newall Green High School

THE DISASTROUS DEVIL

Many moons ago I was riding my horse
In the middle of a long and lonely road,
I felt freezing cold
Then suddenly there appeared a shining light
It was filled with buckets of fright
There gleamed a red demon under the moonlit sky
The lightning sawed the night sky
'Come to the depths of Hell or I will eat your soul!'
He took me to the fiery vault that he called home.
There I will stay for all eternity in agony!

Adam Pate (12)
Newall Green High School

SCHOOL

I love science, it's great fun,
PE and games are brilliant too,
they keep you active.

I hate homework
there's lots to do
and every lesson
you get some.
I also hate RE,
it is boring and makes me fall asleep.

Arron Finch (11)
Newall Green High School

ON THE SCHOOL BUS

When I was on the bus
I was in a mad rush.
I was going to school
what a fool.
I was not on time
and it was a crime.
I feel sad
and also mad
Oh my god, it was a job.

Jack Hawksworth (12)
Newall Green High School

MY FIRST BIKE

I got a new bike
Then went for a hike
I rode like the wind
Through the day
Went any which way
And when I got back
I hit the sack.

Stephen Bird (14)
Newall Green High School

HALLOWE'EN

It's Hallowe'en night.
It's very cold.
Leaves are flying around.
Kids are running around
looking for a good house
which will give them candy.

A lad comes up
taps me on my shoulder
makes me scream.
But now I'm older
when they do it again
I won't feel colder.

Amelia Rigby (14)
Newall Green High School

RAPPER MC REE

Rapper MC Ree
Wanted to borrow a skeleton key
To help steal cars
With girls wearing bras
Go into town
Have a drive around
Rapper MC Ree hopes
He won't get found
Driving fast
In his stolen black Porsche
Listen to the blast
Of some loud music
Trying to impress
Hopes he doesn't lose it.

Rapper MC Ree
Went into HMV
To buy a CD
For his new black Porsche
Driving round the streets
Like a slalom course
Rapper MC Ree
And his skeleton key.

Reon Davies (13)
Newall Green High School

ZODIAC

Brothers are there
always in your hair
they mess up your stuff
until you go buff

Your mum starts to shout
'Is there anyone about?'
my brother is crying
while I am lying

I storm to my room
bing, bang, boom
I moan and I groan
I scream to the bone

I finally go down
wearing my dressing gown
I apologise so much
I sound double-Dutch

My brother's my mate
there's no need to hate
he asks me to play
until the end of the day.

Becky Sefton (11)
Newall Green High School

BYE MUM!

All I want is a kiss goodnight.
For my mum once more to be in sight.
She got ill last year
With cancer to the breast.
She died yesterday, now she's at rest.

I held her hand till she fell to sleep.
I knew she would never wake.
I started to weep.
I loved her so very much.
Now I long for a mother's touch.

Clare Welch (13)
Newall Green High School

DEPRESSION

Depression is the colour of blue,
Depression is known to most of you.
Depression is a painful time,
What you do is cry most of the time.

Just want to be on your own,
Locked up, inside alone.
Depression makes you want to cry,
Depression makes you want to die.

Depression can lead to self-harm,
Just remember to stay calm.

Depression is a black cloak,
Once it catches you,
You begin to choke.
You can't control the thoughts in your head,
All you want is to stay in bed.

Depression, depression, will it get better?
Please help, I am at the end of my tether.
Depression, anger, builds up inside,
To your friends, you confide.

This world not hard to hate,
Friends don't understand, but relate.

Kelsey Latimer (13)
Newall Green High School

MY UNCLE BOB

When an angel passes by
I sit down and start to cry
There's so much I need to say to you
There's so much I need to say and do
I wish I could hear you speak again
The voices around me just don't sound the same
I miss you too, but what am I gonna do without you?

Samantha Farrar (13)
Newall Green High School

A STORMY DAY

On a stormy day,
On a stormy night,
The wind hurtling past the houses,
The world as black as soot,
The volcanoes erupting,
The colour of my friend, Sarah's hair.

Thomas Haspell (11)
Newall Green High School

BONFIRE NIGHT

Bonfire Night is on its way,
Are the children good? Who can say?
Bangers, rockets, Catherine wheels,
No matter what, the rocket squeals.

Little children laugh with joy
All except a little boy
No one has bought him fireworks
What a shame, they're just jerks!

Vicky Hindley (13)
Newall Green High School

CATS

Light-up eyes like lamps
A bendy back, like paper
Teeth like fangs
A tail like elastic bands
Fur like wool
Legs like sticks
I like cats!

Chloé Boswell (11)
Newall Green High School

FOOTBALL MAD

We are the best
We're always at the top
We never move
All the matches I've never missed
Our team is the best
We are
        Manchester City!

Sophie Herstell (11)
Newall Green High School

ME AND MY CAR

Me and my car
My love is given
My car is driven
The engine is smoky
And my throat now is croaky
My car says,
'Are you fine?'
'Yes,' I shout,
'But get me some wine
Oh, and before you go, what's the time?'
'The time, my leader, is ten to nine.'

Klodjana Hasi (13)
Newall Green High School

MY SCHOOL LIBRARY

In my school there is a lovely library
and it is very lively.
Mrs Fildes doesn't mess about,
annoy her and she will kick you out.
The door is open from 3 till 4,
for plenty of people to read and draw.
The computers and Internet
are a fair bet.
So come to the school library.

Joe Farrar (13)
Newall Green High School

My Nana

I miss my nana more than anyone can see
I know she's watching over me
I hope she can forever see
She will always be with me.

I didn't want my nana to die
On that night, I wondered why
All night and day for three days I would cry
I still get upset and that's not a lie.

I remember her chips
Her fag on her lips
Her little wise tips
And her big bag of Skips.

I used to sleep every Saturday
'Never smoke,' she used to say
She's gone away
But in my heart she'll forever stay.

I miss my nana more than anyone can see
I know she's watching over me
I hope she can forever see
She will always be with me.

She died in September
Which I'll always remember
In my life and heart,
She's definitely a member.

Jenna Deveney (13)
Newall Green High School

UNTITLED

We didn't know,
We couldn't see,
These sly little gestures,
Were you telling me?

We saw the bruises
We saw the cuts
Was it her
With the cigarette butts?

She dragged you up
She dragged you down
Was it the stairs
She dragged you around?

You kept it quiet
And all locked up
Until one day
It became too much.

You cut your wrists
Blood came out
But it would not stop
It would not drought.

As you sat and started to weep
You only wished for a peaceful sleep
But once you slept you could not wake
What happened to the life that
              you would take.

Victoria Gough (13)
Newall Green High School

MY MESSAGE

I sent a message
To the fish
And told them
This is what I wish.

I am a witch
With magical powers
I wish my garden
Was full of flowers,

I am the Queen
I'm terribly mean
I wish my house
Was oh, so clean,

I am the bird
Now don't be absurd
My favourite pudding
Is lemon curd,

The little fishes
Of the sea
Sent no answer
Back to me,

This is where I'd
Like to be
So don't go
Calling me,

The little fishes
Gave me a grin
Why, what a temper
You are in!

Jade Dawson & Emma Burns (12)
Newall Green High School

AM I DIFFERENT?

I don't feel different,
So why do you see me this way?
I still have two eyes and a nose.
Is this the way it's always going to stay?

Just because I look different,
On the outside of me,
Is it my colour, my size or weight?
Please help me because I can't see.

You think I'm different,
My background, glasses and brace.
It makes me so unhappy,
That you can't see beyond my face.

I'm not different.
I want to get it through.
We're all the same - on the inside.
Yes, I'm the same as you!

Vicki Bootman (14)
Swinton High School

PREJUDICE

Why are people so racist?
Blacks have done no wrong
Inside they're the same as white people
They just speak in a different tongue

Appearances shouldn't matter
It's what's inside that counts
Men shouldn't be judged by colour
Of that there is no doubt

There are great people all around
Black and white alike
So like the song tells us to
Let us give peace a chance.

Nicola Burke (13)
Swinton High School

FACE

My face is only part of me,
You've got to get to know,
That you're so immature,
You've got to stop and grow.

When that car pulled up beside us,
I thought it would be fine,
But when I saw the drugs,
I had to draw the line.

As we crashed into the road,
I felt myself blackout.
All my thoughts were swirling,
I didn't know what it was about.

I woke up in the hospital,
Wondering what I looked like,
I hoped my face would heal,
My 'friends' could take a hike.

They didn't stand by me,
They didn't understand,
Especially Natalie.
She wouldn't even hold my hand.

You don't realise how much it hurts me,
When you point and stare,
How can I help what I look like?
You really just don't care.

Vikki Jones (13)
Swinton High School

REMEMBER ME

You tease me, you hurt me
Then pretend it's alright
And just another day has passed
When you go home at night

When I come close
You hiss and you jeer
You're deaf to my cries
And I fill up with fear

You thought it was funny
To be a fake friend
And I loved you as long as it lasted
Even though I knew it was pretend

I'm alone in my room
Where I cry all night
Because when you kicked me
You gave me a fright.

I'm alien to you
I mean it, I swear,
You wouldn't notice if I'm green
Or had bright blue hair

So now I ask why
Why aren't you my friend?
While you stand and stare
My life's at an end

It doesn't matter now
For now I'm not here.

Sharron Cheetham (13)
Swinton High School

THE PEOPLE TO BLAME

Why me? Am I being punished for a crime I didn't commit?
I have suffered long enough, and now I am at the summit
Of torture, which you will never see
Because it is happening inside of me.

To understand, it's not so hard
But it's easier to keep me out, like I am barred
From joining in laughing, to blend with the crowd
Not to be smirked at, to be laughed at loud
I may be different, yes, but treated the same
If I am taunted for that, who is to blame?

A blockage, a wall, an invisible barrier
Stands between you and the Asperger's carrier.
For example, facial expressions, easy for you
Sometimes I wish I could understand them too.
I may be different, yes, but treated the same
If I am taunted for that, who is to blame?

Intelligence is another issue,
Being teased for that, why? I don't have a clue.
Everyone is better in different ways than others
A fact that when near me, most of you cover
So they feel it's OK to call, to point, to stare,
How would you feel if you were standing there?

Asperger's is a big thing to bear,
You think, it isn't right to make fun of a person in a wheelchair
Because they are obviously feeling pain
I may not be showing it, but I am the same
Could that dignity extend to me?
It is unfair to call what you cannot see.

Christopher Ogden (13)
Swinton High School